by Sara Jane MacDonald

**Dark and remote, it seemed
to cast a shadow over the new bride's
brightest hopes . . .**

FROM where I sit in the garden, if I turn my head slightly to the left, I can see mountains through the trees. Blue they seem, mist edged — mist which swirls and lifts and dips to hide their craggy peaks: mysterious mist which encloses me in this place, trapped, locked in by mountains and sea.

To my right lies the Gulf Stream, a huge expanse of dark blue water that cuts me off from the mainland. On its surface, small sailing boats scud, fishing boats head in and out to sea and often there are navy frigates.

There's water everywhere. A shallow river that even runs past the bottom of my garden. I'm surrounded . . .

In that river, Greylag geese wait, webbed feet planted firmly like gossiping women in the stones at the bottom of the river, waiting to be fed with bread each morning.

5

Herons as big as ostriches alight in the trees or settle like old stiff men on one leg in the water, waiting for I know not what.

I know they're Greylag geese and herons only because Stuart has told me so. I sigh in the quietness of the garden, sigh crossly at myself as I think of Stuart and his happiness and pleasure in all this.

I know that it's beautiful, this Scottish island he has brought me to. I see and feel the remoteness and peace. The air is clear and pure, but it disturbs me, makes me uncomfortable.

I cannot warm to the excessive and overpowering scenery. It doesn't make me feel welcome, any more than Stuart's friends appear to.

I believe I am as alien to them as they are to me. They view my entry into their closed circle with great surprise and suspicion.

I have been married four weeks and it seems like four years. Each day stretches endlessly before me . . .

The worst part of it all is hiding how I feel from Stuart. As his shift at the hotel ends, I shower, change, paint a cheery smile on my face and prepare intimate, candlelit dinners, the highlight of my entire day.

I can't shatter his dreams. After years on the mainland he's back where his heart is. He has just opened a hotel with his parents and two brothers.

He has worked so hard, he deserves his happiness. If only there was a job for me at the hotel, but as yet there isn't. When, in my first week, I longed to be useful and insisted on going to the hotel with Stuart, it was made obvious, in a kindly way, that I was a hindrance rather than a help.

"Ach, away and enjoy yourself. You've no' even had a proper honeymoon and you'll be wanting to be doing things to your new home."

It's as if by being a townie — a thin, blonde, English townie — I'm not used to or capable of hard work.

So I spend my days alone. Stuart thinks I stride the glens and cliffs, but I find them awesome. I feel self-conscious walking alone and I'm afraid of getting lost.

Even in the holiday season the island absorbs the tourists and they disappear into the countryside as if they've been swallowed.

ONCE, walking along Glen Rosa to the waterfall, with the mountains rising up on either side of me, I felt as if the crags really were going to envelop me and I would vaporise into mist.

I turned with a cry and ran puffing back the way I'd come.

Since then I have walked along the river following the rocks to the town beaches, towards the harbour, where the ferry leaves three times a day for the mainland, its deck crammed with holiday-makers going home.

I watch its progress across the sea. I climb the cliffs and watch until it's only a dot on the horizon, until the sea is bare once more.

The ferry is my only concrete evidence that the outside world still exists. When it's gone from view, I feel bereft.

When it appears again on the horizon and I can hear, or think I can hear, the throbbing of the engines, my spirits rise again imperceptibly.

6

CRAFT
CELTIC CROSS PICTURE

POEMS

Printed and published in Great Britain by
D. C. Thomson & Co., Ltd., 185 Fleet
Street, London EC4A 2HS.
© D. C. Thomson & Co., Ltd., 2002

ISBN 0 85116 817 5

When Stuart has time off, we go to meet his friends. They like to climb and to walk the mountains. They like to play golf and to sail.

I can do none of these things. Invariably, I wear the wrong things, make the wrong moves, blurt out fatuous comments through nervousness and a longing to be liked and accepted.

None of Stuart's friends means to be unfriendly, I know . . . except for Mary. She actually does mean to be unfriendly and I understand her only too well.

She's an ex-girlfriend of Stuart's, and she uses every opportunity to cast up reminders of their days together. She's also a good walker and golfer and she likes to be the centre of attraction with a ready wit that makes everyone laugh.

She touches Stuart's arm a lot and smiles up into his face. When I see him looking down at her and laughing, I go as cold as ice-water. I wonder why he married me and, worse, imagine he does, too.

Ours was such a whirlwind romance. It really was love at first sight. This dark man, with the bluest eyes I've ever seen, walked into the conference centre in London where I worked, and I just stared and stared.

He caught my eye and quite simply stopped in his tracks while people walked around us. And that was it.

We saw each other constantly and when his business course ended 11 days later, he proposed and I accepted — without thought.

Neither of us thought beyond the hot, sun-filled days. Beyond the moment, beyond our noses, beyond our total infatuation with each other. Neither future nor past were real, only the immediate present, the roller-coaster, heady excitement of being in love.

When I remember those days, I'm comforted by their close intensity and Mary fades into insignificance once more. But now, sitting here in the garden, the cold shiver of fear returns with the memory of last night.

A gap is slowly opening between Stuart and me. Did we really have love, the lasting kind — or was it a kind of folly, a dream gone wrong?

Last night, I couldn't sleep, though Stuart lay beside me, breathing evenly.

I lay for a while listening to the silence inside and outside. When it seemed to roll towards me like a dark blanket, I screwed my eyes tight shut against it and pretended I was home in London.

I strained for the sound of traffic, a constant hum in the distance. I listened for the sounds of car doors banging and voices calling out to each other.

I listened for the raucous singing and shouting when the pubs closed. I listened for my flatmate moving around, giggling in the dark.

I heard only the black stillness of a Scottish island sheltered from the world. I heard only the movement of sea all around me, soft, insidious, hissing against the shore, subtle as a snake, barring me from contact with everything I knew and understood.

In one movement, I was out of bed and gone from the room. I

moved carefully in the dark to the back of the house and stared out of the uncurtained window.

There, on the mainland across the black waters, patterns of small orange lights twinkled: inviting; warm; so near and yet too far.

There, people moved and danced, drank and laughed and chatted in a language I was familiar with. There, people worked and relaxed in a culture that I understood.

In that moment, in the dark, I saw all too clearly my mistake. Love just wasn't enough. Stuart and I came from different worlds. I could never be happy here. If I had been a Scot it might have helped, but I was a Londoner born and bred.

I longed for the bright lights and the uneasy, earthly warmth of the city. How could I ever, even in the madness of a first-time love, have imagined differently? I loathed this place.

There, I had admitted it. Loneliness and despair swept over me, and I wept.

I DIDN'T hear Stuart until his arms were around me, holding me, comforting me, stroking me until I stopped shaking and sobbing.

Then he led me back to bed and held me tight until morning. But he said not a word and, in his stillness, I recognised his own despair.

He'd tried to transpose his Cockney sparrow to his homeland, to a place he loved and belonged, and the sparrow had lost her chirp and her jauntiness in doing so and had become just another dreary little bird.

My misery was catching and I wasn't fooling him. My awful, unlovable homesickness was causing the bright colours of our love to fade.

When he left for work, he looked sad, though he tried to smile.

"We'd better have a talk tonight when I come home. You can't go on being this miserable. I hate to see it." And he was gone.

Perhaps when I've left he'll be able to get together with Mary again. They seem a good match. I double up in a spasm of pain. But will she make him happy, I wonder.

I hear the garden gate open and turn to see Morag, Stuart's older sister, coming up the path.

"Hello," she calls. "Am I disturbing you?"

She has her dog with her and another dog on a lead. Jessie bounces up to me, her tail wagging, and licks my hand. Morag sits beside me.

"I'm dog-sitting today. This is Beth, half sheepdog, half Lab, and a wee gem, aren't you, girl?"

I wonder if Stuart has sent Morag. I ask if she'd like some coffee.

"No, thanks. I wondered if you felt like a walk? I thought I'd take the dogs along the foreshore towards Corrie."

It's the first time anyone on the island has asked me to go anywhere. They've all been too busy.

I go inside for my sweater. Even if Stuart did ask her to come, it's nice to have company.

8

"If you could take Beth along the road it would help," Morag says. "We'll let them off as soon as we reach the golf course."

The dog doesn't pull at all. She walks steadily beside me on her lead, looking up at me every now and then as if to assess me.

When we reach the golf course, we unleash the dogs and, released, they bound off quickly. We walk along the edge of the golf course to the shore and then turn to face the castle nestling in the arms of the mountains.

It's a clear day and their peaks are exposed to sky and sea. Morag hums and I'm glad I don't have to make conversation. For the moment it's enough to be with someone.

Suddenly Morag calls the dogs and then points to the rocks in the distance. I can just make out small, sleek heads and feel rising excitement. Putting the dogs on their leads once more, we move carefully forward, closer.

They lie, the seals, awkward and as exotic as mermaids stretched on the rocks, their flippers and heads raised, their smooth, plump bodies in complete contrast to the sharpness of the rocks.

Pups lie beside their mothers, wide-eyed, touchingly beautiful. In the water they swim and bob and play, unaware of us watching them.

I am enchanted. I am captivated. I have only ever seen these sea creatures in a murky pond in a zoo and, as we silently watch them, I realise for the first time the horror of captivity.

Then, as if there has been some hidden, unheard signal, they move, bounce, wriggle deftly off the rocks and slide into the sea, heads disappearing into the waves until they are only black dots on the choppy surface of the water.

I turn away. Morag is watching me, a curious smile on her face. She bends and lets the dogs off the leads. I can't speak. Seeing the wild beauty of seals at such close quarters has rendered me speechless with excitement.

We walk on slowly and Morag begins to tell me about a pup seal they saved when they were children. When he was better, they returned him to the sea, but he would come out of the sea to them when they banged large stones together to call him.

He appeared for years and years afterwards, then one year he didn't come although they banged stones for weeks. Stuart stood and cried his eyes out, not knowing what had happened to him. Stuart had been eight, Morag fifteen.

I enjoy her lilting, soft voice as we walk, telling me of Stuart's childhood.

BACK home, I make sandwiches and coffee and we eat out in the garden. Above us, seagulls cry and fly out to sea in droves to catch the fishing boats.

I want to confide my alienation and loneliness to Stuart's sister but I can't, for it implies criticism of her family's welcome and their way of life.

As if reading my thoughts, Morag suddenly turns towards me and says,

"When I was working on the mainland, in Glasgow, I couldn't settle. I couldn't get the feel of the place.

"I felt slow and dull with all the noise and quickness of things.

She pauses, looking out to sea across to the mainland.

"But I had a good job and a commitment and a wee bit of advice from an old Polish lady who lived above me. She told me, 'Bend your ear without prejudice to the sounds of the place you find yourself in, and you will be excited despite yourself.

" 'For you'll be discovering a strange, new landscape and experiencing completely new surroundings — and how else can we grow to be rounded human beings?' And, of course, she was right."

Before I can say anything, Morag smiles at me and jumps up.

"Heavens, I'm late for the hotel. Look, I can take Jess, but can I leave Beth with you and collect her later?" And she's gone, running down the path.

Beth and I look at each other. She has a Labrador's head and body and the skinny legs of a sheepdog, which make her look like one of those fat ladies who still have shapely legs.

I stroke her velvety ears tentatively and she appears to like it. I get up and take the plates and cups inside and she follows me. I put water down for her.

I decide to do a spot of gardening and she sits beside me and moves around with me as if we've known each other for years. After a while, I find myself talking to her.

Stuart, home early, startles me. By the laughter in his eyes, I know he has heard me talking like an idiot to the dog. I feel myself blush and he hugs me.

"Come away now. The steamer's coming in and we'll have a drink and watch her leave."

"But, Stuart, I can't leave the dog. Morag's coming for her later."

I see the laughter again.

"Bring Beth along. She's well behaved. We can drop her by the hotel later."

It's a lovely evening and we sit and drink and watch the steamer's propellers churning the sea, making for other islands. As I sit absently stroking Beth's smooth, black head, I realise this is the best day I've had for a very long time.

When we reach the hotel, Morag, obviously busy, looks at Beth ruefully.

I say quickly, "How about if I keep her tonight?"

Morag looks relieved. "That would be great of you."

We stop off on the way home to buy Beth food and, once inside, I set Stuart to finding an old rug and box for her to sleep in.

"She's so good," I say with surprise. "What must it feel like to be suddenly left with strangers?"

"Very nice, I imagine," Stuart says drily. "Look at all the attention she's getting. Frankly, I'm jealous."

10

Our eyes meet and we laugh together. It's so long since we've done that.

THE next day, Beth is restless, so I get out a map and trace an easy coastal walk. The following day I pick a longer one and take a picnic, which we share on the cliff top.

I do this, for a week, planning each day with care so Beth doesn't get bored. Still Morag doesn't collect her. Nor the next week, nor the one after that.

One hot afternoon, I'm lying on the cliffs with the harbour behind me, small islands on the left and the mainland before me.

As I lie, I hear the throb of engines through the ground as the ferry noses out to sea. If I sit up I'll see it making for the mainland.

But I don't sit up. I lie with my ear to the earth and other sounds reach me — bees, insects in the grass, voices murmuring on the wind.

There's a dull thudding beneath me, like a heartbeat, as if the island has come alive under my still, listening body.

I sit up and look at the ferry and feel no great pang of homesickness. I look around me. How blue and shimmering the water below me is. How exotic the castle looks nestling in the trees with a backdrop of mountains.

How magnificent those mountains, green, brown, craggy, encased in moving, white, wispy cloud. I turn and see how different each of these mountains is. I must learn their names. I must climb them. I must get to know them.

Beside me, Beth nudges me and whines. She wants to move on. I suddenly realise that's exactly what I've done — moved on apace. I pull her silky ears and hug her.

"You, Madam, were a plant! I don't know who you belonged to, or who schemed you into my life, but you're mine now and I'll never give you up."

As I walk downhill with Beth to my island home, I experience one of those rare, beautiful shafts of utter joy in being alive.

As I walk, I feel the new life within me stir. It's as if breathing in the trees and mountains and sea has enabled me to create life within myself. The burns and waterfalls are entering my bloodstream. The throb of earth and sea is becoming my pulse.

Love is my mainspring. Deep, unspoken, intense passion for the man and now, suddenly, like the sun bursting from threatening dark clouds, for his island, too.

I know there will be sad and bad times when the lights over the water will beckon and waves of homesickness and longing will engulf me. I know this will happen.

But I've chosen now, unconditionally, and I'll not look back or overshadow the bright, rosy colours of my world with homesickness and regret for a lost way of life.

I've found a new world. There's a new life within me. I start to run. I want to tell Stuart, watch his face as I tell him of our child.

Beside me, my dog, with her lolloping gait, runs, too. ■

11

AUNT ELLEN'S

By
Nona
Frances

FAVOURITE HAT

It was beautiful — and so were the memories it brought flooding back.

CAROL pedalled hard against the cold east wind. The wire basket strapped to her handlebars was piled high with vegetables and the Tuesday half-pound of sausages for Aunt Ellen.

It was becoming a little difficult to fit in the weekly coffee and chat that always took nearly an hour of her precious day off work. It had been even longer last week. But that was different.

In any case, there was no-one else to visit — not family, anyway. Ellen was the last of her mother's five sisters, and all the other cousins lived up north. Besides, Carol usually enjoyed their little chats.

Carol sighed and braked as the traffic lights changed to amber and then red. Visiting was the least she could do, as Aunt Ellen refused any offers of help either with the washing — her kindly neighbour took it to the launderette — or with the cleaning. Although not a lot, this was done by the home-help who came twice a week.

Even then, Aunt Ellen insisted on doing all the dusting and tidying, with one hand holding on to her walking frame while she worked.

The lights changed to green and Carol pushed off into the wind, her shoulders hunched over the handlebars, glad of the warmth of her old duffel coat, which she'd buttoned right up to the neck.

The ride took 20 minutes on a good day, and today was far from good. She slowed down for the roadworks that seemed to have appeared overnight, like giant molehills.

An enormous crane was squatting in the middle of the road, its savage teeth open, about to lift, swivel and swoop as if to grab a prize from the traffic that had slowed down to pass it in a one-lane crawl.

13

Carol stopped altogether, deciding to wait until the performance was over, and to give herself a breather. At the age of 48 she could do with one!

At least this roadworks delay would be a bit of news to take to Aunt Ellen. She could dress it up a bit to make quite a story.

Being housebound, Ellen was always hungry for news, tit-bits of gossip, or small talk — anything that made her feel part of the bustling world outside.

Last week they had talked about Tim and June's wedding in the spring. He was the first of Carol's children to be married, and Ellen wanted to share the excitement. Carol let her thoughts drift back, reliving the conversation . . .

"What will you wear, dear?" the old lady asked enthusiastically. "What sort of hat?" That was most important to Ellen, whose own dress sense was impeccable.

Carol smiled to herself. She hadn't the elegance or eye for fashion that Ellen had had in her rôle as an ambassador's wife, spending time in many different parts of the world.

The old family photographs in the battered album at home were full of snapshots of the charismatic Ellen Montgomery, surrounded by friends in countries Carol knew only from the map of the world pinned on Tim's bedroom wall.

She remembered that, in every faded photograph, Ellen seemed to have some inner well of secret happiness that shone through each sepia print.

"'Ere, lady, are you stopping for tea?"

Carol jumped as her thoughts were interrupted.

The young driver of the crane was smiling down good-naturedly. The road was clear now.

"Not today, thanks!" She grinned back, and pushed down on the unwilling pedals. Not far now. The wind was getting stronger.

She was glad she had her woolly hat pulled down over her ears. She laughed out loud. Aunt Ellen wouldn't have been seen dead in a woolly hat!

The flat was on the first floor. It was one of four converted from an old Victorian house that had known days of modest grandeur and genteel living.

The rooms had high ceilings, and the spare room had probably been the linen cupboard!

Last week when they had been talking about the forthcoming wedding, Ellen had insisted on Carol lifting down the hat boxes from the topmost cupboard in the spare bedroom.

She remembered every moment of that afternoon so vividly, as if it were happening now . . .

★ ★ ★ ★

The old wooden stepladder just reached the shelves and Carol wobbled slightly as she reached for the old-fashioned, personalised hat boxes that had been gathering dust for many years.

She took them down one by one, placing them at the slippered feet of Aunt Ellen, who was standing at her Zimmer like an eager child watching caskets of jewels appear from Aladdin's cave.

It had been a mildly hysterical few minutes bringing the boxes down, followed by an even funnier session with Aunt Ellen insisting on Carol trying on some of the hats.

"Perhaps one would be just right for the wedding," she said hopefully.

It wasn't as if there were just one or two hats. Each of the boxes, with its faded satin ribbons trickling from the over-sized bow on the lid, contained hats inside hats, inside hats.

There must have been about 20 altogether, each one with its own glorious tale to tell.

Ellen sat in her upright, padded chair in the large, square, front room, the boxes gathered around her feet like children. She gazed at them with love.

Her eyes, the colour of cornflowers, were looking back . . . back to the years when Carol was a small child hearing her mother say, "Look at this lovely bracelet your Aunt Ellen's sent from India!"

The bracelet was still in Carol's trinket box at home — a cherished memento, a glimpse of another life that she had been privileged to share.

FREEWHEELING down a small hill, Carol's mood was still pensive. *Another life that she had been privileged to share?* She'd never thought of it that way before.

She had glimpsed that other life through the windows of Aunt Ellen's unclouded memory. Vivid pictures of exotic places and people who had disappeared into the mists of time.

After all, Carol thought, who else do I know who has monogrammed hatboxes!

Ellen's hats had come from the most exclusive millinery boutiques of the world. They had been made to match perfectly the suit or dress she had ordered from an equally-exclusive couturier.

Carol had discovered a veritable treasure trove inside the boxes last week. There was a silver-grey cloche with a peacock eye trim; a neat French navy bowler with white edging; delicate, pastel silks; richly-coloured soft felts. So many. So different.

Carol had tried each of them on under Aunt Ellen's watchful eye.

The bike gathered speed and Carol felt the wind whistling past her, as she heard again the excitement in Aunt Ellen's voice as she gave directions . . .

"No, no, child . . . You wear it more . . . Here, let me show you."

Carol knelt down in front of the chair and Ellen's thin hands tipped the brim to a more rakish angle. "There, that's more like it.".

Carol looked in the mirror. The pale turquoise actually flattered her blonde hair. Perhaps she could wear it. It would certainly please Aunt Ellen.

She had turned to say so and stopped. Ellen was looking at the last box.

There were stars glistening in her eyes — or maybe tears.

"Ah, Carol, this one is extra special." Her voice still had a soft lilt. "Shall we take a peep inside?"

Carol carefully untied the flattened, grey, silk bow and gently levered off the lid. Silently they both gazed into the elegant box.

The hat was a truly startling colour — a brilliant cerise, almost electric in its density. Carol reverently lifted the beautiful creation from its nest.

The brim was wide, and gently curved on one side. The straw was fine and expensive to touch, and the delicately-fashioned, tiny flowers, dotted in the curve, spoke of warm summers and lazy days by the river.

Wordlessly Ellen reached out her white, frail hands and Carol carefully placed the hat in them. When Ellen spoke it was in a whisper.

"This was always my favourite."

She paused for a moment or two, gathering her memories around her like a gossamer shawl.

"I wore it the last day we visited Jack at Oxford — it was graduation day. We sat by the river." Her eyes were misty. "It was such a beautiful day."

Carol had not known Ellen's only son. It was so sad. Jack had been killed in France soon after receiving his degree. And so Carol had only ever seen photographs of him.

Ellen was slowly lifting her arms and placing the hat on her thin, white hair. "A mirror please, dear."

Carol hesitated. Perhaps it would destroy the old lady's memories of that precious day."

"There's one in the top drawer," Ellen said firmly, no doubt reading Carol's mind.

Carol brought in the small, gilt-edged mirror and held it for her. Ellen tilted her head to look at the reflection, lifting her chin this way and that until she achieved the desired effect.

She held herself almost painfully erect for a moment and Carol caught a fleeting glimpse of the charismatic Ellen of old.

The elegance was still there. There were some things that time and age could not destroy.

At that moment Carol felt a sudden surge of love for her aunt. Ellen's eyes were bright and her lips smiling.

She was not seeing what Carol could see — she was reliving that unforgettable day in Oxford on the arm of her beloved son.

Slowly the old lady removed the hat and gently laid it on her lap. Her shoulders relaxed into the welcome support of the thick cushions.

Lovingly, Ellen glanced down at the stylish creation she held in her delicate fingers.

"Yes, this was my favourite."

Her eyes were looking far beyond the padded chair, and the gracious Victorian sitting-room. And Carol realised that Aunt Ellen had been reunited with Jack for that precious moment.

Then, with great dignity, the older woman returned to the present.

"Well, Carol," she remarked. "I don't know when I last enjoyed an hour so much. It's been super. Thank you, my dear. Perhaps you could put the hats back in their boxes — except this one. I think I'll keep it out for a while . . ."

THE rain now started to blow through the icy wind and Carol was thankful to turn her bike into Cornwallis Avenue. There was the familiar, blue door.

She parked her cycle against the railings and, taking the bags out of the wire basket, she mounted the four steps into the porch. Then she started up the stairs to the first floor.

A warming cup of coffee with Aunt Ellen would be very welcome. Carol decided to ask if she could borrow the turquoise hat for Tim's wedding. That would please her.

She put down her parcels and felt for the key on the high shelf above the door. To her surprise, it wasn't there. She turned the handle and discovered that the door was open. It stuck as usual, but then it gave way grudgingly as she put her weight against it.

"Hello, Aunt Ellen — it's only me!" Carol pushed the door shut with the back of her foot and walked along the hall.

"Hello," she called again. To her surprise, the bedroom door opened and the familiar face of Dr Morgan appeared.

"Oh . . . Aunt Ellen?" Carol started — but she already knew . . .

"She died very peacefully, Carol. I was here with her." The doctor gently took the shopping from her and sat her in a chair.

"The home-help called me about an hour ago. Ellen seemed to know she was going . . . Are you all right, Carol?"

She nodded and he went on. "There's something else — just a minute, my dear."

He went back into the bedroom and Carol gazed, unseeingly, at the floor, feeling her throat tightening with shock and grief. She heard the sound of his footsteps coming back, but didn't look up.

"Ellen said to give this to you," Dr Morgan said gently. He was holding the cerise hat. "And there's a note. It seems she dictated it to the home-help."

Carol held out her hand blindly taking the folded sheet from the doctor. The notepaper was cream and expensive looking. She opened it slowly and, through her tears, scanned the words.

My dearest Carol,

The cerise hat is yours to wear at Tim's wedding if you feel it's suitable. I just know you'll enjoy wearing it and I do hope it brings you as much joy on this occasion as it brought me on my most special day. Take care always.

Your ever loving,

Aunt Ellen.

Carol looked up through tear-misted eyes. The cerise hat she cradled in her hands seemed to glow even brighter. "Did she say anything else?" she whispered.

The doctor's voice was kindly. "Yes she did, but I didn't understand. She said to tell you Jack had come." ∎

THE ROBIN

Inside the house the fire is bright,
Thick walls protect from winter night.
The children laugh and watch and play
They wish the snow had come to stay.

Night brings sharp frost and bitter chill.
The starving fox hunts for a kill.
Stark trees stand bleak against the sky.
The grass is hidden. Small beasts die.

Perched above the winter stream
Bright the robin's feathers gleam.
Of birds he is the winter king
A promise of a longed for spring.

Joyce Stranger

Inspired by an illustration by Mark Viney

by **Isobel Stewart**

20

My Only Lass

His song was for someone extra special to him — yet it touched so many hearts . . .

IT was an old song and he sang it simply, lovingly, as if there were no television camera or crew, as if there were no-one in the world for him but the unseen girl to whom he was singing these words.

There was a lilt in his voice, a memory of Ireland. His face was lean and brown. He wasn't particularly good-looking, but when he smiled, there was a warmth and a charm in his features that went straight to the hearts of women of all ages.

He was smiling now, as he sang.

"And when I grow too old to dream, I'll have you to remember."

There was no studio audience and he stood quietly as the last notes of the song died away.

"Well, now," he said to the cameras and the smile was in his eyes as well, "I wouldn't say I'm too old to dream, not by a long way.

"But when that time does come, I'll be thinking of the words of this song. And I'll be remembering.

"I'm not saying who it is I'll be remembering, or who I'm singing this for, because she knows. Isn't that the truth, my only lass?"

HE'S singing it for me, Maureen thought, bemused. After all these years, and all that's happened to him during that time, he still remembers how it was.

Oh yes, Kevin, I do know. You used to call me your only lass in just that way, long ago.

She stood up, and switched off the television set. Twenty years ago, a girl of 16 and a boy of 17 had held each other close, and he had kissed her tear-wet eyes, and they had promised to wait for each other.

"I'll be back for you, my only lass," he had said to her, in his voice that was so-newly deep.

It had been a golden summer, she remembered. They had known, the two of them, before school ended, that something strange and wonderful was happening to them, something beyond the easy, casual friendship they had always had. Both their fathers worked on the same farm, and the cottages they lived in were right next to each other.

She'd been wearing a pink cotton dress, that last day of school. It had been handed down from her cousin Bridget, and it had been too big for her, but her mother had taken it in.

Maureen had known, as she had peered into the kitchen mirror, that the rose-pink suited her dark curls and the roses in her cheeks.

"Are you pleased we're finished with school, Maureen?" Kevin had asked her, as they had walked home across the fields.

"Well, I am and I'm not," she'd said seriously. "I'm glad I won't be starting work at the big house until September, but I'm thinking, Kevin, that we'll not be seeing each other too much, for you'll be helping your da in the fields."

"I will that," Kevin had agreed, smiling.

She'd thought there could be no-one in the whole world with a smile like he had, and a warmth like that in his dark blue eyes.

"But I'll get away whenever I can, and we'll see each other," he'd promised.

Maureen had been glad, then and later, that her mother had said she needn't take a job, this last summer, although she would have to help with the cooking and with the younger children. But she had always been free when Kevin came.

Once, as they'd run across the field together, her hand in his, Maureen had looked back and seen her mother, small and still, at the door of the house, watching them.

It had been the river they would go to, most of the time, and when they'd reached it, they would take off their shoes and paddle in the icy-cold water that had run brown over the stones.

Afterwards, they would sit on the bank, and his arm would be around her, and she would lean back against him.

It had been beside the river that Kevin had kissed Maureen for the first time. When his lips had left hers at last, he'd held her close to him.

She'd heard the beating of his heart, and she had thought, then, that she would never, in all her life, forget the wonder of that moment . . .

NOW, 20 years later, she stood in her bright little kitchen, looking out at the neat rows of vegetables in the garden, and her breath caught in her throat as she remembered. We were young and we were innocent, she thought, that golden summer.

"My only lass," he'd murmured, his lips against her hair for a moment before he'd kissed her again.

22

She could remember, as if the years between had never been, the breathless wonder of that summer, the feeling — a foolish feeling, she had known even then — that it would go on for ever.

Then, suddenly, the summer and the magic were over.

The clouds had been grey in the sky the day he'd come for her. He'd been walking, not running, and Maureen had known right away that something was wrong.

"My da's been given the sack," he'd said bleakly. "We're leaving right away, because there's a chance of another job for him."

The long, enchanted hours that had slipped away so slowly through that summer suddenly rushed past so quickly that from being a few days, it had become no more than a few hours before they were due to part.

"We'll write, my only lass," Kevin had said none too steadily.

Maureen had been unable to answer, because of the hurt and the tightness in her throat.

He'd kissed her, then, for the last time, and he'd looked down at her, as if he would take the memory of her face with him.

"I'll be back for you, my only lass," he'd said abruptly, then he was gone.

At first they'd written fairly regularly, but before Kevin had been gone a year, their letters had drifted to a stop, and she had met Nick.

Maureen and Nick had married a year later.

And here I am now, Maureen thought, with a daughter the age I was then, and wondering where the years have gone.

She had seldom thought of Kevin, other than with a faint regret, after she'd met Nick. Sometimes, in these last 10 years, as his name, his face and his voice became well known, she had felt proud to have known him so long ago.

Nick would sometimes tease her about her first love, but it was a teasing they could both smile at, secure as they were in their marriage.

It's a lovely thought, Maureen told herself, that Kevin remembers me, and that he sang that song for me.

If Nick had been in the house, she would have gone and told him, but there was only Jenny, and she had shut herself in her room — once again.

THINKING of her daughter, Maureen could feel the warmth fade. With Jenny being the only one, they had always been close friends as well as mother and daughter — until now.

Since young Dave had left, neither she nor Nick could get close to Jenny.

"I'll leave school," she had told them defiantly. "I'll go to London, too, and I'll get a job. You'll not keep us apart."

"We're not trying to keep you apart, Jenny," Nick had said, his voice reasonable. "Dave has been transferred, and none of us can do anything about that.

"We're very happy for him to come and stay with us whenever he can — and you can write. But we do insist that you're to finish school before there's any talk of going away."

There had been a storm of tears then.

"You don't understand," Jenny kept on saying to them in the weeks since Dave had gone.

You don't understand.

But I do understand, Maureen thought now, with certainty. Because you sang that song for me, Kevin, because you remembered. I remember, too, what it's like to be young, to be in love, and to face a parting.

Now I can talk to Jenny, really talk to her. It isn't going to change anything — she still has to finish school — but she'll know, now, that I understand what she's feeling, what she's going through.

She made a pot of tea, poured two mugs, and carried the tray through the hall. Balancing the tray, she knocked on her daughter's defiantly-closed door.

"Can I come in, Jenny?" she asked. "I've brought some tea."

"I don't want any tea," Jenny replied, her voice just on the right side of politeness.

Maureen took a deep breath.

"I want to tell you something," she said firmly. "Open the door, Jenny."

After a moment, she heard the key turn, and the door opened. Jenny's eyes were red, and her soft mouth was mutinous.

Maureen's heart went out to her daughter.

"I want to talk to you, love," she said. "Really talk. You say I don't understand, Jenny, but I do. I — I'd forgotten just how well I understand."

She put the tray down, and sat down on the bed beside her daughter.

"You see, Jenny," her voice warm with love, "I've been there, too."

H E'S singing for me, Clare thought with surprise. He's remembering me — and he's telling me that he remembers.

Through the years since they had parted, she had wondered if Kevin ever thought about her. As he became more and more well known, when she listened to him or when she watched him on television, she would find herself wondering how it would have been if she had made a different choice all these years ago. Not regretting anything, just — wondering.

He hadn't changed, not really. Clare had watched him through the years, and she had seen a strength and a maturity come to him, but even tonight, as he sang, she had seen in him the young man she had known.

Twenty-three he'd been when he came to work on her father's farm. She had been two years younger.

Until the young Irishman had appeared, Clare had been content with the pattern of her life stretching ahead of her predictably and pleasantly. She had lived at home, and worked in the library of the small market town nearby.

Farm life was all she had known, and all she had ever wanted. She had been due to marry Rob in a few months, and would move to his father's farm after the wedding. Then her father had taken on extra labourers for the harvest, and from the first day she had been aware of the tall, young Irishman with his dark hair, his lean, sun-browned face, and his blue, blue eyes.

Rob, with his fair hair and grey eyes and his clear, clean features, was better looking, but when Kevin had smiled at her, a sheaf of harvested corn in his arms, in the top field, she had been lost.

Clare had always taken her holiday at that time, to help her mother with the extra work of harvest, and each day she would carry the sandwiches and vacuum flasks to wherever the men were working.

She had always done this, and she had never been shy with the men, taking their teasing lightly and easily.

But the Irishman hadn't teased her. He had smiled, and sometimes his hand had brushed hers as she'd handed him a mug of tea. But he had said hardly anything.

Then there came the night, when the harvest moon had been full . . . She had gone out into the garden, and found him there.

She could have turned back, but she hadn't. Instead, she had walked towards the tall figure outlined against the sky.

"They say you're promised," Kevin had said abruptly.

"Yes, I am," she'd replied.

SOMEHOW there was nothing strange in the way they'd begun to talk, as if they were not strangers and never had been strangers.

He had asked Clare about Rob, and she had told him how long they had known each other and of their plans to marry. She had asked him about his singing, and he'd told her that the farming work was only to earn enough money to give him freedom for a few months, to see if he could earn his living with his guitar and his voice — to prove himself.

After a while, they'd stood in the moonlight in silence. Then, as if he couldn't help himself, he had taken her in his arms and his lips had found hers.

And as if she couldn't help herself, her arms had clung to him, and her lips were warm under his.

"I didn't mean to do that," Kevin had said at last, unsteadily, "and you promised to someone else. But now that it's done, I can't say I'm sorry — for I'm not."

Neither am I, Clare had thought with certainty, but she hadn't said it.

There had been only a week of the harvest left, and most nights they'd met in the garden. Clare had said nothing to Rob, partly because it was a busy time for him, too, and they saw little of each other, but mostly, because she hadn't known what to say.

She would sit in the small, quiet library, and look at Rob's ring on her finger, and she would think of the plans they had made over their years of friendship and then courtship.

Then she would think of the Irishman's blue eyes looking down at her, and the warmth of his lips on hers.

The night the harvesting was finished, Kevin had asked her to go away with him.

"We could have a grand life, my only lass," he'd said eagerly. "We could travel the world, and I'll sing for our suppers. Say you'll come with me, Clare."

Afterwards, she thought that she had always known what her answer would be, known it from the moment she'd met him.

"No, Kevin, I can't," she'd told him steadily, sadly. "I couldn't hurt Rob, and my parents, and his parents. I love him dearly.

"That must sound strange, after — after you and me — but it's true. Besides, I couldn't live that kind of life. I'm a country girl, a farm girl."

He hadn't tried to make her change her mind. And so she'd said goodbye to her Irishman, and married Rob. There had never been a moment in all the years when she had doubted that she'd made the right choice.

It was good to know, though, that Kevin remembered and that he had sung a love song to her, and he had said, "My only lass" just as he had all these years ago.

She loved Rob dearly, and she knew he loved her — but there was surely something very special about a man who would sing love songs to you.

CLARE switched off the television, smiling a little at her own thoughts. Rob would be in soon. He would be sorry the children were asleep, but he was late, as he often was in the lambing season.

"Clare, open the door for me, love," he called.

She hurried to the back door. Rob was waiting for her to open the door, and there was a newly-born lamb in his arms.

"One of the ewes had twins, and she didn't want this one," he told her, coming into the warmth of the big farm kitchen.

"If it hadn't been so cold, I'd have let this one take its chance with one of the other ewes, but it's bitter. Will you look after it, love?"

Every season, there was a lamb to be cared for, to be brought to her. She took the little creature from him and carried it over to the warmth of the fire.

"There's a bottle in the cupboard beside the sink," she told him, absorbed in the lamb. "Jilly wanted it for her dolls, but I said we might have a lamb needing it."

She warmed some milk and fed it to the lamb, amazed as she always was at how the tiny animal accepted the bottle.

"Can I wake Jilly and Peter, to come down and see?" Rob asked softly.

"They could see in the morning," Clare pointed out, but she smiled. "All right, then, but you can get them back to their beds afterwards."

"I'll do that," he promised.

She turned back to the lamb again, but when Rob didn't go right away, she lifted her head and looked at him.

He was watching her, and her breath caught in her throat. All the love in the world was in his eyes, in that moment before he turned to go up and wake their children.

No, she thought, Rob doesn't sing love songs to me, he lives them. He lives them when he makes sure I have wood for the fire, when he mends the leaking tap, when he makes this big, old house snug against the wind.

And when he brings me a newly-born lamb to care for.

All these things are his love songs to me, and that is something I'll always treasure.

Oh no, Linda thought with certainty.

Oh no, Kevin, I'm not falling for the sentimental approach.

She switched off the television set angrily, decisively.

My only lass, indeed.

The biggest mistake we ever made, she told herself, as she had done so many times before, was to get married.

In the end, that was the only thing they could agree on — that their marriage had been a mistake. It hadn't taken them long to see their mistake, no more than a year or two. But by then, there was Katie.

Because of Katie, they went on trying and trying, until the only sensible and realistic thing for them to do was to admit their mistake, behave like civilised people, and each go their separate ways.

Linda walked across to the window, to the view she loved, the city spread beneath her, the lights twinkling like a carpet of stars.

She had been trying not to think about Katie tonight.

Restlessly, she moved around the flat. It always seemed so quiet, so empty, when Katie wasn't here.

Somehow, Katie had remained a sunny-natured, very normal little girl, accepting, most of the time, that her mother loved her and her father loved her, even although they didn't find it possible to live together.

Or even just to be together, Linda thought now. That was a pity, for she knew Katie would have loved the three of them to spend a little time together.

"Like a real family," she would sometimes say wistfully.

But she would accept it when Linda explained to her that Mummy and Daddy always seemed to argue when they were together, and they knew that made her unhappy, so it was better for them not to see each other.

Why, in these recent months, had Kevin been suggesting they should try again?

"We're older and wiser, my only lass," he had said quietly. "I miss you, and I miss the three of us being together — like a real family, as our Katie says."

But she hadn't returned his smile. She had pointed out to him how foolish and unrealistic he was being — reminded him of the tension and the unhappiness.

"It wasn't like that all the time. Surely there were times when we were happy, Linda?" he had said.

She had looked at her watch then and said, abruptly, that she had to be at a meeting.

Kevin hadn't given up, though. Since then, he had telephoned her, at home and at work. He had written to her and he had sent her flowers.

And now this — singing to her, and smiling to her like that, and calling her his only lass in that special way he had . . .

As she moved about the quiet, empty flat, restless, unable to settle, Linda found herself remembering what he had said — "We're older and wiser now." She was also remembering the song he had just sung to her.

"When I grow too old to dream, I'll have you to remember."

Linda stood still. It's true, she thought, I'll always have him to remember. And there were happy times for us . . .

*   *   *   *

Kevin had taken her to Ireland soon after they had been married. He hadn't been well known then, just starting to get a few singing engagements, hoping to make a record.

She'd been only a junior secretary then, with her hopes, too, of becoming personal assistant to the fashion buyer she worked for.

Then, Katie had been a baby and Kevin always bathed her.

If I shut my eyes, Linda thought now, with an ache of memory, I can see him kneeling beside the bath, his sleeves rolled up. I can hear Katie laughing. I can see myself, standing in the doorway, smiling at the two of them.

They had gone to Paris together, when Katie had been two, leaving her with Linda's sister. Already, they had been feeling a tension between them, a strain, but that week had been magic.

They had been walking on the Left Bank one day when the rain had come on suddenly.

A young couple on a scooter had stopped beside them to take shelter and, completely unselfconsciously, they'd taken off their crash helmets and gone into each other's arms.

When the rain had stopped, they'd drawn apart, put on their crash helmets and gone on their way.

"That was the best way I've ever seen to make the best of the weather," Kevin had said softly.

They had walked across the Pont Neuf, her hand in his, neither noticing nor caring that the rain had begun again.

The problems had come in the years after the magic of that moment — the demands of her job, and what she wanted, and the growing demands of his fame.

LINDA realised only now that she hadn't considered the possibility of their trying again. Now, with the flood of memories released, she found herself wondering.

She walked across to the phone and then she changed her mind.

She thought again of the song he had just sung. If we don't try, that will be all we'll have — memories.

She knew where he would be now. She would go to him and tell her that she would like to try again.

And they would take it from there.

When Kevin Sullaven left the studio, he drove straight to the hospital.

They had said he could see Katie, although it was late, and her bedlight was still on, in the small side ward.

She was propped up on her pillows and her blue eyes — his eyes, Linda had always said — were bright, although her skin had that translucent look that tore at his heart.

"Well now," he said, bending over to kiss her, "and how's my girl tonight?"

"I'm fine, Daddy," she replied. "You did it, like you promised. You sang the lovely song for me."

"Sure I did, my only lass," he said not quite steadily. "Are you all set for tomorrow? Is Dr Morrison having an early night to get himself ready?"

Katie giggled.

"I told him you said he was to do that, and he said he'd try." She nodded, and a little of the brightness left her eyes.

"I don't really like operations," she said a little shakily, "and I don't like being in hospital, but Dr Morrison says we have to do this one."

Bone-marrow transplant. The words had sent a chill to Kevin's heart. But there was no choice.

As the doctor had explained, with the transplant, there was a chance for Katie. Without it . . .

"Is Mummy coming tonight?" he asked carefully.

Katie shook her head. "She was here this afternoon and she says she'll be here when I wake up tomorrow."

"Of course." Linda had timed her visit so that she wouldn't be here when he came.

HE looked at his small daughter, her eyelids heavy now.

"Go to sleep if you want," he said softly. "I'll sit beside you for a bit."

"The nurse gave me a sleeping pill," Katie explained. "But I'm not sleeping yet, Daddy. Sing to me, please."

He sang to her softly, the old songs she loved, his head close to hers on the pillow. Neither he nor Katie heard the door open, but when he finished, he looked up to see Linda standing beside him.

"Mummy!" Katie said joyfully. "You came back."

Linda bent and kissed her.

"Yes, I came back," she replied.

There was something in her voice that made Kevin look at her again, unable to keep the question and the hope from his eyes.

"Are you going to stay, too, Mummy?" Katie asked.

Linda sat down on the other chair.

"Yes, love," she said steadily. "I'm going to sit here with Daddy, and even if you fall asleep, we'll stay until Sister tells us we have to go."

Katie looked from her mother to her father.

"Will you both be here tomorrow, when I wake up?" she asked. "Together? Like a real family?"

Kevin saw Linda hesitate, but only for a moment.

"Yes, Katie," she said steadily. "Just like a real family." ■

AND BABY

MAKES THREE...

by Carol Marsh

But sometimes three can be a crowd — as Steve was beginning to find out . . .

"GO on, Steve," Liz urged, over the baby's feeding bottle. As her husband hesitated, she nodded impatiently at the telephone in his hand. "Tell David you'll come. It'll do you good to get out for a while."

"But . . ." He had been going to say, "But what about you?" Before he could utter the words, however, Liz had hoisted the tightly-wrapped, white bundle against her shoulder, and was gently patting his tiny back.

"Now, precious," she said soothingly, "let's see if you have any more nasty wind."

Steve sighed, feeling, not for the first time, right out of things. "OK, Dave," he said quickly into the receiver, "I'll meet you in the pub in twenty minutes."

As he stepped through the baby paraphernalia that seemed to have completely taken over the house, he glanced at Liz. Her face was soft and contented. She smiled at him, almost absently, over the baby's downy head, and his insides melted.

"I won't be long, love," he promised. "Only David's not in town all that often, and . . ."

"Don't worry!" Liz had lowered little Alex skilfully on to the changing mat and was kneeling over his wriggling, half-naked body, giving him her undivided attention.

She didn't even seem to realise how odd it felt for Steve to be going out without her to meet a shared old friend, like David.

Then, pushing aside any misgivings, he went up to their room to change, but even then he felt a pang of guilt as he splashed on some aftershave.

It still felt strange kissing Liz goodbye and brushing Alex's unbelievably soft, delicate cheek with his lips.

Then a sudden thought came into his mind as he closed the front door behind him. He remembered being single and living at home and never thinking twice about leaving his mother behind to handle the domestic side of things.

David was waiting in their old stamping ground leaning against the bar chatting to a very pretty blonde barmaid Steve didn't remember seeing before.

"Congratulations, mate!" David exclaimed, coming forward and holding out his hand. He looked slightly embarrassed at his own formal gesture as Steve walked over to greet him. "What'll you have?"

"Half of bitter, thanks, Dave." The well-ordered bar was so different from the chaotic room he'd just left.

He sat on a stool and watched as the barmaid pulled the beer, and David placed it, with great ceremony, in front of him.

"Well, fancy you being a father!" Dave went on, shaking his curly head in wonder. "How are they both anyway?"

"Oh, fine — they're both fine, thanks, Dave." Steve was surprised at how much that "both" grated — as if further emphasising what he had known, right from the beginning — that Liz and Alex were a natural, inseparable pair.

He swallowed, and as David grinned encouragingly, obviously waiting for more details, he heard himself say, "He's a great little lad — a bit on the small side yet, but coming along well."

Alex was on the small side, being premature, but not even the bossy district nurse, who'd been visiting them since Liz came home from hospital with Alex, had prepared Steve for the way he felt about the tininess, the vulnerability, of his son.

AS David chatted, bringing Steve up to date about his job and his own wife, Susan, Steve tried hard to relax and to listen attentively.

But there was something inside that wouldn't allow him to be completely at ease. And he realised, in a wave of almost physical pain, that it was entirely owing to the fact that he wanted Liz there beside him. He wondered what she and Alex were doing now.

He picked up his glass and took a swig of beer. As the door opened and closed and several couples drifted in and out, he frequently glanced round expectantly. He knew it was pointless but he couldn't help himself.

As if reading his thoughts, David said, "I suppose Liz'll be out of action for a while now, with the baby and everything."

Out of action doesn't describe it at all, Steve thought bleakly as he nodded automatically.

On the contrary, since Alex had arrived, Liz had seemed to swing *into* action. Brisk. Efficient. Totally in charge of the minute human being who was a part of him too, but who had thrown *him* completely off his guard.

As David turned to talk to some other friends, Steve's thoughts strayed again as he reflected on the joy of meeting Liz nearly five years ago now, when they were at college together.

"We'll be together for ever, darling — share whatever comes our way." He blinked as he recalled her words the night he asked her to marry him.

"I know we're young and everybody thinks we're crazy!" he'd ventured breathlessly between kisses, "but we love each other so much, we'll make it work, won't we? Promise me, sweetheart."

"Wake up, Dad! I said, do you want another drink?" David's laughter broke into his thoughts.

Taking his friend's empty glass, Steve said, "My round," vainly trying to match Dave's cheerfulness.

At the counter, the blonde barmaid smiled and held his gaze for a moment as he handed over the money. For just a second, excitement flared inside him before he tore his eyes away.

He thought of Liz smiling like that; invitingly and not preoccupied with the baby — a more slender Liz, her make-up beautifully and skilfully applied — her hair loose and shining, not always tied back to keep it out of Alex's eyes.

Liz before Alex . . .

More guilt washed over him, as he sought yet another memory of Liz, fresh and lovely, flinging herself into his arms last summer, shouting ecstatically, "I've been to the doctor's for the result, darling! It's positive!

"Oh, Steve, we're going to have a baby — at last."

A baby — of their own. He couldn't imagine it, even though they had talked, and hoped, for such a long time. The planning and waiting had, like everything else they did together, been an absolute joy.

Steve sighed almost wistfully now as he thought of those nights when he and Liz had lain in bed, and she'd taken his hand, and placed it gently on her abdomen.

"Did you feel that kick?" she whispered, her blue eyes full of the mystery and wonder of it all.

If only, Steve thought in spite of himself, if only the reality had been anything like the promise!

He took the drinks over to the table where Dave was now sitting with several people. The conversation was lively and full of laughter, and occasionally he found himself drawn into it, but he still missed Liz.

But as the evening passed slowly, thoughts of Liz kept coming again and again into his head. He remembered the night when, quite unexpectedly, he had woken to find her in pain.

"Quick, Steve!" she'd gasped, clutching at his hand. There was panic in her voice. "Something's wrong! Ring the hospital!"

From that moment, everything seemed to have been taken out of their hands as the medical team stepped in and, because of complications, it was some time before he learned that his wife and child were both well.

"Oh, Steve!" Liz had whispered tearfully, a little dazed from the traumatic events of the last few hours, as he bent, heart thudding fearfully, over her fragile, hunched figure. She'd clung to him as he'd tried to comfort and reassure her.

Then, brimming with love and pride, she'd wiped away the tears and asked softly, "Have you seen him yet, Steve? He — he's so perfect, so beautiful!"

IN spite of his promise to be home early, it was late by the time Steve left the pub and said his goodbyes to David.

He hadn't had a lot to drink, but his head was reeling from the noise and laughter, and his own sense of isolation.

Now, after thinking about Liz virtually all evening, he suddenly didn't feel like hurrying home. She would probably be in bed, anyway, he thought, with Alex tucked up snugly in the cot beside her.

The thought made him feel lonelier than ever.

She'd made it clear enough before he went out that she wasn't really bothered whether *he* was there or not!

Almost defiantly he forced his key into the lock and pushed the front door open.

At that moment, he heard the noise — the ear-splitting sound of the baby screaming!

"Liz! What's wrong?" he called anxiously.

Forgetting everything, Steve leapt up the stairs two at a time, and stopped dead in the bedroom doorway.

Wearing an old dressing-gown, and with a towel round her obviously wet hair, Liz was pacing the floor with the squalling baby in her arms.

She turned, her face white and tear-stained, as Steve lumbered in.

She took one look at him then, to his astonishment, thrust the baby into his open arms.

"There!" she exclaimed, her voice breaking in a fresh vale of tears.

"You have your son — I've had enough!"

Steve opened his mouth to speak, but no words came out. He looked down at baby Alex, lying for the first time completely unsupervised in his arms — as tiny and vulnerable as he could possibly have imagined.

He is my *son*! he thought, in dawning wonder and amazement. Part of me. And at that moment, Alex stopped crying, hiccuped, and pushed an amazingly tiny fist into his mouth.

At the same time, as if she had been returned to him from a long journey, he realised that Liz really needed him.

"You told me to go," he reminded her softly.

"I know . . . I know." She sobbed and suddenly, she was in his arms, and he was holding her, as well as the sleeping baby. "But I never knew I'd miss you so much and — hey, you're wearing aftershave!"

Steve grinned, lifting her face with his free hand to look deep into her eyes.

Surprise and relief washed over him. "Only a splash!" he said playfully.

Gently, Liz took the baby without moving out of his embrace. "I think *he* missed you," she said softly. "He's been crying all the time you were out."

"Really?" Fresh pride welled up in Steve as he leaned over and touched Alex's other tiny hand. Immediately it opened, and his finger was enveloped in a remarkably strong grasp.

In answer, Liz kissed him, the towel on her head slipping to her shoulders to reveal her nearly dry, still shining hair. "I'll go and put the kettle on," she said quietly. "Then, if you like, you can give him his bottle — it's about time you learned!"

And as she handed Alex over, and turned to go out of the room, Steve realised, with joy in his heart, that the future had really begun. ■

SIX SUPER TROUPERS

by Dorothy Ashley

> **Against all the odds, the boys — and their faithful dog — turned a show-stopping disaster into a glittering success.**

JANE paused just long enough to read the large notice pinned on the outside of the twins' bedroom door — she didn't want to be caught standing outside their closed door again.

The notice read, **IN CONFERENCE! NO ADMITTANCE UNDER ANY CIRCUMSTANCES! NO LISTENING OUTSIDE THE DOOR!**

The last bit, she was sure, had been added for her benefit and she hurried on, but not before she had also seen the footnote in small print, **Beware of Dangerous Dog.**

Dangerous dog, indeed! Jane made a face at the empty basket in the kitchen as she walked in.

Lancelot was one dog who would never make a name for himself as a guard dog, the young softy.

Not for the first time, Jane wondered what her sons were up to.

When the five Hammond boys huddled together in private — and went around the rest of time looking as if butter wouldn't melt in their little mouths — their mother sensed trouble.

"It's Christmas, my darling — the time for secret gatherings and whispered conferences," her husband had replied cheerfully, when she had voiced her misgivings before he had left for the office that morning.

He had given her a mischievous grin that reminded her of the twins when they were up to no good and tapped her lightly on the nose with his newspaper before picking up his briefcase.

His last words before shutting the door behind him were, "No prying!"

That's all very well, Jane fretted, as she set about preparing the boys' elevenses.

She felt certain, though, that this secret had nothing to do with Christmas presents because William and Victoria Robinson, from next door, were also involved.

She split some newly-baked scones in half and picked up the knife to butter them, when the phone rang.

Several minutes later, Jane returned to the kitchen with a thoughtful expression on her face and finished buttering the scones.

She put some milk on the stove to heat and nipped out into the hall. "Elevenses in the kitchen for those who want any," she called up the stairs.

There was a sudden clatter of feet up on the landing as the boys tumbled over each other to be first in the kitchen.

L ANCELOT trotted in too, looking very smug because he had beaten them all, followed by Joseph, the youngest of Jane Hammond's brood.

She smiled fondly at him as she rushed past her. Her *baby,* she thought wistfully — although she wasn't allowed to call him that any more.

"I'm four, now," he reminded her loftily when she tried to mother him, "and I'll be going to proper school next year."

The twins came down next, their round faces flushed with exertion, or heat, she wasn't sure which.

Her "double trouble", Jane called Richard and Matthew, for they only looked like a pair of heavenly angels with their blond hair and blue eyes.

Nine-year-old Thomas was right behind them. He was the charmer of the family and, like his father, was already adept at twisting poor, unsuspecting females round his cute little finger.

Jane felt quite sorry for Victoria whom, she suspected, had been given a task in whatever scheme her boys were plotting at this moment, that none of *them* wanted to undertake!

The twins had been born on Thomas's second birthday and, sometimes, Jane felt it was like having triplets, they were so much alike.

Jonathan was the last one to come down. Jane resisted the urge to give him a quick hug, as she knew he wouldn't appreciate it.

They chatted as they munched and Jane asked if William and Victoria were coming round. "Yes, Mum — later," Jonathan answered briefly – he wasn't giving anything away.

"Oh, by the way," Jane said nonchalantly, "your grandmother rang up a few minutes ago.

"She's coming over a few days earlier than planned, so I want you to clear your room, Jonathan, and put the Z-bed up in the twins' bedroom."

She almost choked on her scone when the boys stopped eating and stared, open-mouthed, at her.

Lancelot, with a nervous glance at the five horrified faces, slunk off in the direction of his basket.

Graham's mother came every Christmas and the boys always looked forward to the day Grandma arrived.

Jane narrowed her eyes and said, "You're all looking as lively as a wet weekend all of a sudden.

"I thought you were looking forward to your grandmother coming to stay. She'd be really hurt if she could see your faces now!"

They all hastened to say they were happy about Grandma coming, looking across the table at Jonathan at the same time.

Two spots of colour flamed in his high cheekbones. "It — it's just not convenient at the moment. I don't have to do it today, do I? There's plenty of time . . ." he tailed off bleakly.

"Don't argue, there's a dear! Just so as I ask," she said impatiently. "I've got enough to do without leaving the beds until the last minute."

Her son's reaction to such a simple request was quite out of character.

Jonathan had been given many privileges as the eldest. As a very special one, which had pleased him very much, he had been given the small guest room at the top of the stairs, on his eleventh birthday.

But it had been on the understanding that, if visitors came, he would have to move out, which he had agreed to do quite happily, at the time.

The boys now finished their snack in silence, exchanging odd looks with each other and Jane felt quite relieved when William and Victoria walked in through the back door and they all went upstairs together.

When the boys came down for lunch, Jane was fully prepared for further arguments.

She was quite taken aback, therefore, when Jonathan told her he had cleared out his room and made up his bed in the twins' room.

FOUR days to Christmas — and the air in the Hammond home hummed with activity, as festive decorations were hung, with much noise and laughter, and gaily-coloured wrapping crackled behind closed doors.

The boys went less often to the Robinsons' house after their grandmother arrived and Jane was pleased.

The house had seemed only half alive, without their noise and chatter.

They were going to take Lancelot to see Albert Watkins at the Nightingales Rest Home after their mid-morning snack and the twins were grooming the reluctant hound while Jane looked on sympathetically.

Lancelot was far from the scruffy puppy the boys had presented to her all those months ago and she loved him as dearly as they did.

Albert Watkins was Lancelot's former master but, when he feared he would have to have his puppy put down because he could no longer care for him, the boys had begged to be allowed to have him.

Graham came home in the afternoon with the Christmas tree and the older boys helped him decorate it.

Joseph sat with his grandmother, making a Christmas table decoration.

The tree was put up in front of the french doors at the dining area section of the large room.

Jane leaned her head against the back of her armchair by the fire, happily watching them.

Graham was arranging the fairy lights over the branches and becoming a little impatient now and then with the twisted flex.

"I thought you were going to buy a new set of lights this year," she murmured.

"I was, but I forgot," her husband replied shortly and Jane picked up her knitting, telling herself to mind her own business!

At the end of a hectic day when the boys had long since gone to bed, followed soon after by their grandmother, Jane yawned and said she might as well go up, too.

Jane was almost asleep when Graham joined her in bed. She turned her head to give him a hasty kiss, before dropping right off to sleep.

IT was some hours later, when Graham sluggishly emerged from a deep slumber and, with a loud groan, turned over to switch off the alarm clock.

Then he realised that it wasn't the alarm that had woken him but Lancelot's persistent barking outside the bedroom door.

He drew back the bedclothes, muttering to himself, "Why tonight, Lancelot?" as he reached for his dressing-gown.

The acrid smell of burning when he opened the door sent him flying down the stairs, almost falling over Lancelot as they both tried to reach the bottom first.

Lancelot went straight to the lounge door where smoke could be seen rising from under the edge and growled.

"Good boy," Graham whispered as he passed him and cautiously opened the lounge door at the further end.

He stepped over the threshold and caught his breath sharply when he saw the Christmas tree burning.

He dashed back into the hall and collected the fire extinguisher from the cupboard under the stairs.

At the same time, he shouted to Jane to get the family out of their beds and into the kitchen.

When he was sure there was no likelihood of any further fire breaking out, Graham opened the french doors to clear the air.

Then Jane, holding Joseph by the hand and with the rest of the family close behind her, walked slowly into the room. Her husband couldn't meet her eyes as they rested on him, after she had silently taken in the wrecked tree, the charred curtains and the scorched ceiling.

THOMAS broke the awful silence. "What are we gong to do now, Jon?" he asked.

The boys were unnaturally quiet, exhibiting none of their usual excitement when faced with the smallest of dramas and Graham felt unnerved.

He raised his hands, palms upward. "I'm sorry . . . I — it will all be cleared up before Father Christmas climbs down the chimney," he joked half-heartedly.

No-one smiled.

"It will be too late then," Jonathan mumbled, staring bleakly at the chaos before him.

His mother looked puzzled and, with a quick glance at his younger brothers, Jonathan went on to explain their plan in jerky sentences.

With the help of William and Victoria, they'd planned to put on the Nativity Play in the lounge, with the tree and its shining star in the background.

The play had been scheduled for Christmas Eve afternoon.

"It was to be a special treat," he went on, "for you, Dad, the Robinsons and Grandma, as a thank you for all you've done for us over the past year.

"We've been rehearsing in William's room since . . ."

He gave a side-long glance at his grandmother and hastily continued, ". . . and we've made our own props which we've stored in his bedroom.

"Now . . ."

Lancelot, sensitive as always to his young playmates' moods, thrust a wet nose into Jonathan's hand hanging limply down by his side.

Jane's knuckles were pressed white against her mouth. She took her hand away and said huskily, "We'll do our very best, boys, I promise you, to get the room tidied up by the afternoon."

Graham made a tentative suggestion that, should it be necessary, they could put the play on in the Robinsons' house.

Jonathan shook his head. "Their house is too small," he said.

Later, Graham went out to buy another tree and his mother took the boys into town to purchase new decorations and lights.

After lunch, Jane went off to see Albert Watkins, taking him his Christmas present.

Graham and the boys were left to get on with decorating the new tree.

Graham was up the ladder hanging fresh curtains at the french doors, when Jane burst into the room, still dressed in her outdoor clothes.

"Where are the boys?" she cried, her face flushed with excitement. "I have something to tell them."

JANE awoke on Christmas morning to the sound of soft giggles coming from the twins' bedroom where, she supposed, all the boys had congregated to investigate the contents of their stockings.

She stretched and smiled happily. What a lovely Christmas this was going to be — it had started so well!

She turned her head but it was too dark to see her husband's face on the pillow beside her and, as he didn't speak, she let her thoughts drift contentedly to the events of the previous afternoon at the Nightingales Rest Home.

It had really been so kind of Matron to suggest the boys put their play on in the residents' big lounge, where a huge Christmas tree stood, like a beacon, in one corner.

"They'll love it," she had promised Jane, when she overheard her telling Albert about the fire and the boys' disappointment.

She had been right, too, Jane told herself. The play had been a great success.

Jonathan had played the part of Joseph and his Mary had looked up at him so adoringly as she rocked her new baby in the crib beside her.

William had been the inn-keeper and one of the three wise men, with the twins as the other two — and Thomas had been the narrator, standing all by himself on an upturned box.

The boys had worn their own woollen dressing-gowns and colourful headsquares, borrowed from various female relatives, anchored in place with circlets of white cord.

Jane grinned in the darkness as she recalled wondering, at the time, where they had got the cord from?

But her expression softened as she pictured in her mind the last scene, when the smallest worshipper had walked into the stable leading the "donkey".

There wasn't a sound to be heard in the audience, not even a muffled cough as Lancelot, wearing a brown mohair jumper belonging to William's father, and sporting a pair of large cardboard ears above his own soft floppy ones, humbly bowed his head, in homage to the new King.

That dog, Jane thought, not for the first time, is a saint the way he allows the children to get away with things no self-respecting dog should allow.

Dear Lancelot! She smiled. He might not be the most beautiful dog but he had proved himself a wonderful companion.

She felt her husband stir beside her as he made a move to get out of bed. "Careful, darling," she whispered. "Don't lose your pyjama trousers!"

Graham switched on the bedside lamp and turned to face her. "Do you know, there wasn't one pair in my chest of drawers with a cord in the waistband," he said plaintively.

Jane chuckled. Her boys hadn't grown haloes yet! ■

by Suzanne Thorpe

They were strangers with nothing in common — except memories of the same hotel suite.

Double Booked!

G OING back to Sorrento?" Louise's mother gasped.

"And on your own, Mum!" Emma echoed, with equal shock.

Louise smiled to herself — she had expected such an outcry.

"But, Mum — have you any idea what Latin men are like? They'll chase anything female!" Emma reminded her.

"Thanks," Louise said, feigning a hurt note in her voice.

"Oh, I didn't mean —"

"Don't worry, love!" Louise chuckled. "I do know what you mean about passionate Latins — even with forty-five-year-old widows! But I'm intrigued as to how *you* found out, especially as your only trip to Italy was the school one to Rome?"

That quietened Emma.

41

"And I have been to Sorrento before, remember? Many times," Louise went on.

"But that's just it," her own mother cut in. "That's where you and Don went for your honeymoon, and for holidays before Emma was born."

"I know," Louise said, realising she could never hope to explain to them all the new, and often frightening, feelings her early widowhood had aroused.

Best not even try to explain that for two years she had mourned Don, while he and their life together had become a subject that was mentioned only in hushed voices. Suddenly she had had enough of it.

Don had enjoyed his life, and their marriage had been a happy one. She had found herself wanting to celebrate those things — to remind herself of them and not cloak herself in forgetfulness and grief.

Louise was also filled with an irrational and overpowering urge to return to Sorrento — to be precise, to the Vesuvius Suite in the Majestic Hotel, where their marriage had started and all their holiday memories had been.

She wanted to do silly, delightful things like wear a wide-brimmed hat, gain a tan and put a flower in her hair, drink champagne and watch the sun set from her balcony.

She also wanted to savour their memories and no doubt shed a few tears, but also smile a few smiles. All she wanted was to start living again — to plunge into life again at the deep end.

"I've made up my mind . . ." Louise said.

HARRY was feeling uncomfortable in the coach as it wound its way from the airport at Naples to Sorrento. He had never done anything this reckless before — at least not since he had married Jean on the rebound.

Part of him had known it wouldn't work, but it had at least lasted 10 years, he reminded himself gloomily. Now he was cramped and crumpled from an economy flight . . . and from the ruling of his divorce settlement . . .

If only he had married Angelina . . .

As the pink and white villas flitted by the coach window, he half expected to see her at one of the pavement cafés. He had never forgotten her, and as the years rolled by, her image had grown brighter and more beautiful as his marriage grew emptier.

Angelina, the dark-eyed laughing Italian girl he had fallen in love with when working for his shipping company in Naples. Angelina, whom he proudly called his very own Sophia Loren — if only he hadn't tried to pressure her into marrying him after just six, sweet months.

Later, he realised her Sicilian family would only have countenanced a very long and chaperoned courtship — that he had simply been too impetuous.

How could he ever forget waiting in the Vesuvius Suite of The Majestic with a chilled bottle of champagne, waiting for Angelina to arrive and then elope with him? It seemed like only yesterday when he had waited in the rain, when the champagne had grown warm, and his heart cold.

Why was he going back? How many times had he asked himself that, and been unable to answer? Perhaps it was because Sorrento and the Bay of Naples were where he had spent his happiest times, and because now he was all alone.

"The Vesuvius Suite?" The receptionist looked flustered. "I was just trying to explain to the signora here — it is, er, it is not available . . ."

Louise had been at the reception desk for all of ten minutes. She was feeling hot and untidy after her flight and couldn't understand the delay.

She had, after all, written in advance to book the suite, and now there was a rather pushy, frowning man in a suit asking for it, too.

"What's the problem?" A man in a smart, brown suit appeared at their side.

"Both the signora and the signor want the Vesuvius Suite," the receptionist explained.

"And you are not together?" he checked, looking at Louise for an answer.

"Certainly not!" she snapped back, while the man at her side mumbled something inaudible.

"I am Luigi Rossi," the brown-suited Italian introduced himself. "I am the manager of The Majestic. Would you both come with me, please? How long it is since you stayed here?"

As Louise accompanied Signor Rossi — and the man in the creased suit — she felt her heart rise quicker than the lift. It was racing ahead to the blue and gold upholstery of the Vesuvius Suite, and its shutters which opened like wide-flung arms to the bay.

But she sensed, too, the growing excitement on the face of the man. What on earth does he want with that suite, she wondered irritably? Another disturbing thought chased it — what did she . . .?

At last they were approaching the double doors of the suite, and although its impressive gilt sign was missing, its doors were still cornflower blue and ornately carved.

Signor Rossi opened the doors wide, and for one frozen moment Louise felt her features set. Then her heart sank, right to her sandalled feet.

"I'm sorry," Signor Rossi was saying. "It has been partitioned off. To the left is a twin room with bathroom, and to the right, as you can see, is the fire escape.

"New regulations, about five years ago. I must apologise that you weren't informed of the alterations."

Louise gave a sidelong glance at the man in the crumpled suit. He

43

looked as disappointed as she felt, but his face then relaxed into a smile.

"Harry Morgan," he announced, unexpectedly offering her his hand. "I'm sorry I've been so grouchy!"

"Louise Fletcher," she offered back. "It's quite all right."

"Would you — er — let me buy you a drink?" he asked. "Later, of course, when we've solved the problem of accommodation. With it being early in the season, that shouldn't be difficult for Signor Rossi."

SORRENTO had changed little in other ways. It was still as beautiful, perched on its sheer pink and grey cliffs over a sapphire bay.

It conjured up vivid memories for Louise and, it seemed, for Harry, too, although he was reluctant to talk about his. Both were glad, though, of the other's company.

"I must have talked your ears off!" Louise laughed, on the fifth day of the holiday.

"And I must have walked you off your feet," Harry countered, "but I've really enjoyed it. I hope it hasn't been too painful for you, though. I mean, reliving all the things you did with Don?"

"No," Louise said without hesitation. "I've wanted to relive those memories — and make some new ones, too."

She glanced around them, at the little square, bleached white in the sun where they were drinking wine and resting in the midst of a guided tour of Capri.

THE air smelled of dry heat and the tang of the orange trees around the café, where Louise has been feeding the little fish hors d'oeuvres to a stray cat under the table.

Suddenly she wanted to reach out to Harry — if only to pat the hand of this warm and patient man, so unlike the frowning, crumpled one she had locked horns with on arrival. She did, she decided there and then, want to get to know Harry Morgan.

"Harry, forgive me if I'm being rude, but you've never said why you came back here, why you wanted the Vesuvius Suite, too.

"And I couldn't help but notice how well you know the area."

But Harry was distracted by something across the square, even though he started to answer. "I suppose I returned to relive a dream, a beautiful dream . . ."

His face was alight with curiosity.

"Would you, er, excuse me, Louise?"

With that Harry left the table and strode into the square, where an Italian woman was struggling to quieten a gaggle of five boisterous children.

She half turned and in the strong sunlight Harry couldn't fail to recognise the features, even in profile. Yet they were fuller, the figure much stouter, the hair scraped back severely and the once-laughing face claimed by a harassed frown.

44

As she turned to face him, he found himself turning away from the strange, new Angelina, before she might recognise him.

Across the square, Louise was waiting for him, and her lovely, intrigued face was a welcome sight.

"Just someone I used to know," Harry said in explanation.

Before Louise could probe further, the travel guide was clapping her hands and herding them away to the Villa of St Michele, perched high above Capri.

"The Sphinx of St Michele," the guide's voice announced over a bunch of heads, "is supposed to grant all good wishes if you touch its tail. I made a wish here once — to return to Capri. A week later I landed this job! I now return every day!"

A little impressed "ooh" rippled through the group, then most wandered on to browse through the garden.

Only Louise and Harry lingered, looking at the sun-baked, stone Sphinx, as it crouched on the wall, gazing out into the infinity of the Mediterranean and, beyond, North Africa.

"I suppose that's just like life," Harry mused.

Louise gave him a questioning look.

"To give us what we want, but not always in the way we expect it," he explained.

"Well, I don't think I should miss the chance to make a wish!" Louise decided on a happier note.

And as she leaned over the wall to touch the Sphinx's tail, Harry thought how lovely she looked, as bright-eyed and hopeful as a teenager. He also couldn't remember when he had felt quite so contented . . .

"What did you wish?"

Louise smiled playfully. "Now, Harry — if I tell you — it won't come true, will it?"

But the tender smile Harry gave her spoke louder than any words and said, "It will if I've anything to do with it!"

Signor Rossi came to the reception area to say goodbye to them personally.

"Maybe next year you will both come back to Sorrento?"

"Oh, well . . ." Louise began.

"We hope to, yes," Harry said.

As they both walked out to the airport bus, Louise whispered mischievously to him, "I'm sure he still thinks we came here together!"

Signor Rossi and his receptionist watched them go.

"Maybe next year," Signor Rossi said, "we can show them the *new* Vesuvius Suite across the courtyard!"

"You mean . . . ?"

"Yes, I mean that next year I don't think they'll be fighting over it." ∎

CELTIC
CROSS PICTURE

The rich Celtic tradition of images and stories has provided the inspiration for our delightful cross stitch picture.

The stitched design is 58 x 58 stitches, approximately 10.5 x 10.5 cm (4¼ x 4¼ inches).

YOU WILL NEED
* Fabric: 14 count Aida fabric in cream, 20 x 20 cm (8 x 8 inches)

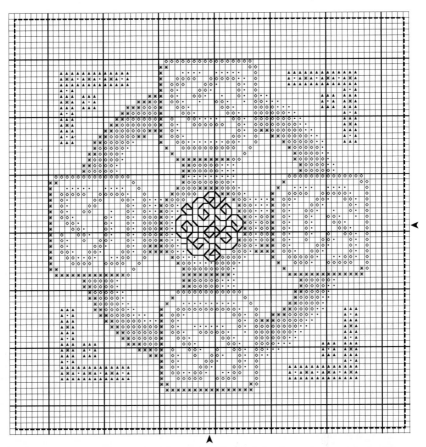

* Thread: DMC 6-strand embroidery thread in the following colours and quantities:

Symbol	Colour	Shade	Skeins
✴ Dark Stone	Dark Stone	646	1
◇ Mid Stone	Mid Stone	642	1
• Pale Stone	Pale Stone	648	1
▲ Green	Green	470	1

* Tapestry needle: size 24
* Card mount: in brown
* Masking tape
* Wadding (optional)

STITCHING INSTRUCTIONS
Cross Stitch: Use three strands of embroidery thread
Backstitch: Use two strands of dark stone
Mark centre of material with running stitches
Starting Point: This is marked on chart by arrows

MAKING UP

Iron the embroidery on the back on a thick towel. The dotted lines on the chart indicate the placement of the mount aperture. Buy or make a card mount to fit the size of your chosen frame. Here the aperture size is 13 x 13 cm (5 x 5 inches) and the outside measurement is 20 x 20 cm (8 x 8 inches). Centre the fabric carefully within the mount, trimming the Aida if necessary, and secure to the back of the mount with masking tape. It is very effective to pad the embroidered area slightly. To do this, cut a piece of wadding slightly smaller than the aperture. Cut a piece of card the same size as the aperture. Place the wadding over the back of the embroidery and the card on top of the wadding. Tape into place.

VARIATIONS

This design would also make a charming cushion motif. All you need do is mount it on a plain cushion cover and edge with toning braid.

● Taken from CELTIC CROSS STITCH by Anne Orr & Lesley Clarke, published by new Holland Publishers (UK) Ltd.

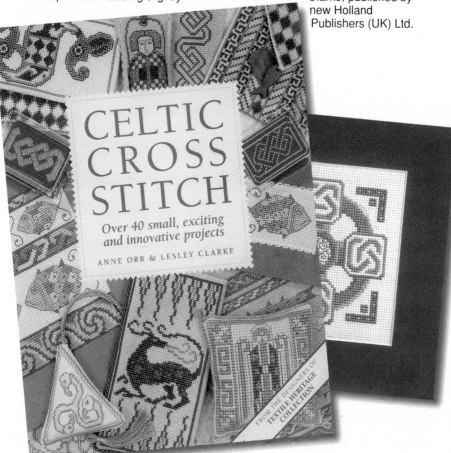

48

Your Verses

The corner where readers share their thoughts

A SPECIAL BIRTHDAY

A ring of lighted
candles, excitement
fills the air,
the birthday host is
seated in the
topmost chair.
Each gift is opened
swiftly, and
gratitude expressed,
with a smile
bestowed upon each
and every guest.

The cake is
decorated with icing
white as snow,
embroidered with a
message so
everyone will know
the laughing host
who clearly is
having so much fun,
has reached the
golden age in life,
of a hundred years
and one.

*Ann Rutherford,
N. Yorks.*

OUR DAYS

Each new day is a
gift
To start our lives
again,
To learn from each
new yesterday,
The sunshine and
the rain,
The pleasures and
the sorrows,
The things which
touch our lives,
The people whom
we meet
And like, dislike and
leave.
All these contribute
to the way we live
Our lives today,
tomorrow.
Thus it is we never
should
Forget that
yesterday
Gave birth to our
tomorrow.

*Diana Morgan,
Tunbridge Wells.*

ONCE IN A LIFETIME

Rich cream flowing
satin,
Sleeves falling from
Milk white
shoulders.
Slim waist with sash
of blue.
The dress is new.
Cream veil that
Grandma wore
Held in place by a
borrowed coronet,
That sparkles in the
sunlight.
A once in a lifetime
day,
The church is cool,
Filled with the
perfume
From the many
flowers
That decorate this
sacred place.
Her bridegroom
waits
For her, his bride.
Today is theirs, to
make their vows
To leave this place
As man and wife.

*Jill Bennett,
Cornwall.*

49

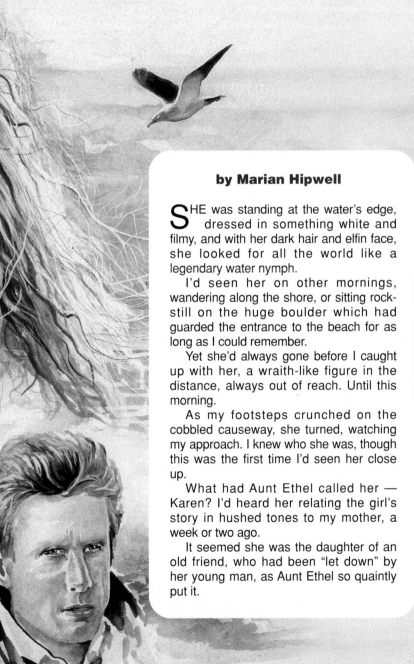

by Marian Hipwell

SHE was standing at the water's edge, dressed in something white and filmy, and with her dark hair and elfin face, she looked for all the world like a legendary water nymph.

I'd seen her on other mornings, wandering along the shore, or sitting rock-still on the huge boulder which had guarded the entrance to the beach for as long as I could remember.

Yet she'd always gone before I caught up with her, a wraith-like figure in the distance, always out of reach. Until this morning.

As my footsteps crunched on the cobbled causeway, she turned, watching my approach. I knew who she was, though this was the first time I'd seen her close up.

What had Aunt Ethel called her — Karen? I'd heard her relating the girl's story in hushed tones to my mother, a week or two ago.

It seemed she was the daughter of an old friend, who had been "let down" by her young man, as Aunt Ethel so quaintly put it.

Apparently she'd taken it rather badly — so badly, in fact, that she'd been sent here, to our quiet little village, in the hope that she would, in these tranquil surroundings, "get over it."

Judging by the dark hollows around her eyes and the sadness within them, her family's hopes had so far not been realised.

"You'll get your feet wet," I told her.

"I like getting my feet wet," she replied shortly.

There was a defiant note in her voice, which dared me to question her presence here at this hour, or make it any of my business. And that was fine by me.

All I wanted was a quiet day on my own in my favourite place.

She was looking out again towards the horizon, and I followed her glance to the dark mass of land a mile or two from the shore.

"It's called Monks' Island," I told her, anticipating her thoughts. "Though the monks are long gone and there are only birds there now. That's where I'm headed this morning."

Receiving no acknowledgement, I shrugged and wandered past her towards the jetty, where my boat was moored.

As I threw my gear into the boat and loosened the mooring rope, I could feel her gaze upon me.

When I turned round, she was still watching me and there was something in her eyes, whether she knew it or not, which wouldn't let me go sailing off to Monks' Island leaving her there alone.

"You can come with me if you want," I called to her, but my voice sounded brusque. "That's if you can trust a stranger," I tried to smile reassuringly.

"Not that I am one, exactly. The lady you're staying with is my Aunt Ethel."

I hoped she'd refuse, tell me she didn't need my pity, particularly now that I'd made it plain I knew who she was. I'd give her one more chance.

"You'd need to go back to the house for more sensible clothes. Oh — and it might be an idea to leave a note for my aunt so she won't worry about you. I'll wait ten minutes."

She looked at me uncertainly for a moment. Then she turned and sped lightly back the way she had come. I sat waiting in the boat, feeling foolish.

Had I frightened her away? Her emotions, after all, were what my aunt would describe as being in a "delicate" condition.

Or perhaps her silent departure was her way of telling me what she thought of my offer.

Still, I'd said I'd wait ten minutes . . .

WELL within that time, I saw her running back down the beach. Moments later she'd scrambled into the boat and seated herself across from me, her expression again daring me to say I'd changed my mind.

"I'm Tom," I said, trying to be friendly.

She didn't volunteer her name. I'd already indicated that I knew who she was, and there seemed nothing else she wanted to add to that.

We didn't talk much during the sail over to the island; I was too preoccupied with rowing the boat and she seemed content just to sit there, looking across the water with those eyes which seemed to see both everything and nothing at the same time.

When we landed, she did make an effort to help, though, pushing hesitantly at her end of the boat as I dragged it up on to the shore.

It was still early and she shivered suddenly in the cool air, despite the thick anorak she'd put on.

"Do you come here a lot?" she asked, glancing round.

I nodded. "I like to get here early — before the tourists."

"And do you watch birds all day?" she asked curiously, making it sound as if it were the oddest way of passing time that she'd heard of.

"It's an absorbing hobby," I said defensively. "And if I do feel like a change, there's always fishing. Or I might go for a swim. It's very relaxing here."

At that she fell silent and sat gazing out to sea. Even now, I was still wondering at myself for inviting her along — and at her for accepting.

She seemed content to be left to her thoughts and as it seemed unlikely she'd suddenly turn into a chatter-box, I reached confidently for my binoculars. In fact, after a while, I almost forgot she was there. She was so still and quiet, I thought she must have fallen asleep.

When I looked at her some time later, however, her eyes were open, staring at the birds with such intensity that I wondered if she was really seeing them at all, or was lost in some private, painful world of her own.

From time to time we made polite conversation, and, gradually, I felt a sense of companionship settling over us, after the awkward start.

Why I'd burdened myself with her — a stranger, and one with problems too, I still didn't know.

But now, at last, this peaceful place seemed to be weaving its own particular magic; she no longer had that blank look in her eyes.

I T'S a lonely place, this." She spoke suddenly. "Don't you feel that?" I considered the question carefully. "It could be," I said at last. "But I can't help thinking that loneliness is something inside yourself. If it's there inside you, you'll feel lonely anywhere."

I could feel her eyes on me then. "You're quite at home here," she said, dodging the issue.

But I knew what she really wanted to know. *Is it inside you, the way it's inside me?*

I suspected, too, that she would have felt better if I could also have admitted to feeling that emptiness inside.

"I've never felt lonely here," I confided at last. "But then, it's a familiar place. I've been coming here since I was a kid. I even spent the night here once, curled up in my little tent." I smiled at the memory.

"I was twelve, and as the night wore on and the wind howled, I got scared.

"Around three o'clock in the morning, my dad came to see if I was OK.

"He knew I'd stick it out, you see, no matter what. So he stayed here with me, instead."

"He sounds nice, your dad." She spoke hesitantly, sensing, perhaps, that the memories were becoming too personal to talk about to someone I hardly knew.

"He's dead now," I murmured. I was glad she didn't offer the usual condolences. Her silence and bent head were more eloquent than empty words ever were.

We had settled ourselves in my usual spot — a sheltered crevice in the rocks from where there was a good view all round, but which also kept out the worst of the elements.

I hadn't bargained on having a guest when I made up my picnic lunch, but we shared what there was. Anyway, she had the appetite of a sparrow.

"What's that?" She pointed to a bird circling high overhead.

I squinted upwards.

"A heron," I informed her. "And that's a kingfisher!" I pointed to where the flash of blue was diving towards the sea." Must be lunchtime for him, too."

She shuddered. "How cruel."

"What's the difference between him helping himself to a fish and us tucking into roast chicken or cod and chips?" I pointed out. "Anyway, life is cruel, sometimes," I added unthinkingly.

"Yes." It was the faintest of whispers.

I'd been thinking of a father, taken before his time, and the broken-hearted boy he'd left behind.

Yet when I looked at her, I realised that she'd put a different interpretation on my words. I had to say something then, to take away that anguished look in her eyes. I think, even if it had been a lie, I would still have said it.

"I do know all about that lonely feeling you were talking about before. Although I don't have it now, it doesn't mean I don't know how you feel.

"When my dad died, I felt lonely. Here. Anywhere. Everywhere."

I caught her arm, so that she had to turn and look at me.

"It does go away, Karen, believe me. You may find it hard to imagine now, but it does fade eventually, I promise you."

When she drew away from me, I realised, in my clumsy efforts to help, that I'd intruded too far into her pain.

She wasn't ready to have that world of hers invaded — not by me, anyway.

She kept her face averted from me as she scrambled to her feet. "I'm going for a walk."

"OK." I didn't argue. "Be careful on the rocks."

I watched as she darted away, a slight figure among the rocks, a flash of colour here and there as she wandered around, trying, I guessed, to come

54

to terms with the emotions which our conversation had aroused in her.

Sighing, I turned my attention back to the birds. There was only so much anyone could do to help . . .

To my surprise, she was back within minutes, tugging at my sleeve as I concentrated on the scene before me through my binoculars.

"There's an injured bird down there among the rocks," she panted. She was breathless from scrambling back over the rocks, and her face was tinged pink.

"Where? Show me."

Scrambling to my feet, I followed her to the spot where a young gull lay, fluttering its wings fearfully as we loomed over it. Gently I stretched out my hand to examine the bird, while Karen watched anxiously.

"Will it be all right?" she asked after a moment. Catching the note of concern in her voice, I looked at her and saw the glistening of tears in her eyes. Something in her expression made me feel that she needed to cry for that bird, because she wasn't able to cry for herself.

"If it had a bit of outside help, it might be all right," I told her.

"But *we* can help it, can't we?" she asked anxiously. I took a closer look.

"Well," I said doubtfully. "It's going to need a lot of care. It might be kinder if we put it out of its misery . . ."

She looked at me then, and I flinched from what I saw in her face but I knew if I were to be of any help to her I mustn't relent.

Bending down, she scooped the bird up into her arms.

"I'll take care of it, if you won't." Her voice was muffled when she spoke. "I have all the time in the world."

Then, by tacit consent, we made our way back to the boat. The spell of the island was broken and we seemed to have nothing more to say to each other.

She sat with the gull in her lap for the whole of the journey back to the mainland. It had made one fluttering protest when she picked it up, then settled, trustingly, against her body.

When we reached the jetty, she gathered the bird to her, protectively, as I leaned down to help her from the boat.

"Good luck with it," I muttered feebly after her. "Aunt Ethel will know what to do. I'll look in to see how it's getting on."

I turned to collect my things from the boat, and when I looked round again, she was running towards my aunt's cottage, the bird clutched tightly to her.

M Y footsteps were hesitant as I made my way to the cottage the following Saturday. It had been a busy week and I'd had no time before now to check up on how things were with Karen and the gull.

I'd thought about them, though, many times.

She was sitting in the cottage garden, amongst sweet-smelling roses, when I pushed open the gate.

"Hello." She smiled and her greeting was friendly enough for me to wonder if she'd forgiven me.

"Hi, Karen," I returned. "How's your patient?"

"The wing is mending," she told me. "Come and see."

Carefully, despite the gull's protests, I examined the injured wing.

"You've done a good job." I smiled at Karen approvingly. "Though he doesn't seem too grateful."

She had been watching me closely.

"I'm grateful," she said softly. "Unlike the gull, I don't mind admitting it."

"Oh?" I busied myself gathering the bird up into my arms.

"Don't pretend you don't know what I'm talking about," she said shyly. "I know what you did."

"I did nothing," I protested. "You did it all."

"I asked Aunt Ethel about you," she persisted. "And she told me some interesting things about you. That you're a park ranger in a nature reserve, for instance."

"So?" I murmured.

She spoke quietly. "A man who spends his life caring for Nature's bounty wouldn't leave a bird to die.

"You acted like that to force me into doing something about my own life — to give me something else to think about, instead of my own problems. You did, didn't you?"

I concentrated on the frightened bird in my grasp.

"Did it work?" I asked at last.

Not that I really needed an answer. There was an air about her, if not exactly one of contentment, then of knowing the worst was over and she was on her way back.

That loneliness, that feeling she had talked about on the island, was still there, but it was less acute, I sensed.

She hadn't believed me when I'd said it faded eventually, but I felt she did now.

We took the gull down to the beach and released it, watching as it flapped its wings tentatively, until, gaining in confidence, it soared into the air.

"Perhaps we should have taken it back to the island," Karen suggested anxiously.

"Perhaps," I replied. "But I'm taking a chance on it finding its way back when it's ready."

Sure enough, the gull circled for a while, then headed off, unerringly, in the direction of Monks' Island. I looked down at Karen.

"We could go across there, if you like," I offered. "That's if you want to make sure the gull's all right."

"I'd hoped you'd take me again before I left," she told me with a little smile.

"Left?" I looked at her, hoping my face didn't show my disappointment.

"I'm going home tomorrow," she said quietly.

"Oh." I was surprised by the extent of my own dismay. "Then it had better be today."

THIS time there was no cool breeze when we landed on Monks' Island. The weather was perfect, as if it knew this was our last visit together and had put on its best show for us.

"Look!" Suddenly Karen pointed excitedly to where a small gull had perched itself on a rock some way off. "Is that our gull, do you think?"

I looked across at the creature now being joined by a group of rather similar looking gulls.

"I'd take a chance on it," I said recklessly.

She seemed satisfied then, curling herself up into a little hollow in the rock, and I turned my attention to bird watching.

"Everyone thinks I was jilted, you know," she said suddenly, some time later.

"Oh?" I smiled encouragingly at her. She sounded as if she wanted to talk.

"I was the one to call off the wedding, actually," she continued after a moment.

I nodded. A look of surprise crossed her face.

I shrugged. How could I tell her that no man in his right mind would jilt a lovely girl like her?

"But it doesn't make it any easier." Her voice trembled slightly. "I loved him, you see. Even though I knew we weren't right for each other, I still loved him.

"And facing up to the fact that we were making a mistake — well, it sort of overwhelmed me for a while . . ."

And now you're fit to fly again — and you're flying away from me . . .

"And — and, as you said, sometimes it take a bit of outside help. Thank you for that, Tom." She looked at me warily.

"That's what I'm here for," I said awkwardly.

Then, in an attempt to be more light-hearted, "Broken wings, broken hearts, I'll have a go at mending them all!"

The words sounded flippant, yet, in my clumsy way, I was trying to tell her something. And I think she understood.

Later, on the jetty, I stood looking down at her.

"Will you be coming back?" I asked, trying to keep my voice even.

"I hope so." She eyed me pensively. "Will you still be here?"

"I'll be here," I told her. *Still looking for wounded creatures to care for . . .*

Standing on tiptoe, she kissed me quickly, her lips brushing my cheek . . . it was like the flutter of a gull's wing against my skin . . .

She turned then, running lightly across the beach in the direction of Aunt Ethel's cottage.

Overhead, a gull circled, squawking plaintively, and I looked up at it.

"She'll be back," I told it, my heart light. "She'll be back . . ." ■

I REMEMBER

When wintry days are dark with gloom
   Seated in my lonely room,
Imprisoned daily in my chair
Waiting help from those who care.

They see me old and worn and gray.
They pity me my endless day.
They do not see that I am free
For memory is left to me.

I stand upon the mountains high,
Looking at the arching sky.
At rocks and grass and heather sweep,
At sunlit crags and crevasse deep.

Forgotten is the daily pain,
For here once more I'm young again.
Hours each day I now can share
With my much beloved mare.

I'm back with her that summer day
My mother sent me out to play.
Not mine at all, but I pretend
She is now my treasured friend.

Forbidden paddling in the stream,
And then I'm sure I'm in a dream.
A miracle has come to pass.
Her foal is lying on the grass.

She turns her head and looks at me,
As if she says 'just come and see.'
I marvel at his perfect form,
This little one, so newly born.

Those who help me into bed
Don't see the pictures in my head.
I have no wish this boon to share.
I sleep, and dream of foal and mare.

Joyce Stranger

Inspired by an illustration by Mark Viney

A VOYAGE OF

by Marian Hipwell

For the three sisters the cruise was a holiday of a lifetime, but the husbands they left behind didn't see it that way!

IT was a good idea. At least, the girls thought so. It was their husbands' reactions which worried Sandra. Not hers, of course — Jack's response to her announcement had been predictably generous.

"It sounds great, love," he'd mumbled from behind his newspaper. "You go ahead. A cruise will do you good; all three of you."

Bless him, she thought tenderly. Not from him the hysterics and tantrums her sister, Jane, was probably facing, right at this moment . . .

* * * *

"You're going where?" Richard eyed Jane incredulously. She could, she reflected, have just announced she had been selected for the next Olympics.

"On a cruise." She spoke patiently. "For eight days."

Richard seemed to be having difficulty in understanding. "But why?" he asked at last.

"Why?" Jane gestured vaguely. "Because I haven't been well and it will do me good. Because Sandra's invited me."

"But we could go on a cruise together, if that's what you want!" he interjected.

"We can't afford it, love," she said patiently.

"Neither can Sandra!" he was quick to point out.

"She's had a small windfall," Jane explained carefully.

"Well, surely she could buy a new carpet or something with it?" he responded, frowning.

"She *could*," Jane agreed. "But she's decided to do this with it. With Jack's full blessing, of course. Really, Richard."

A sliver of irritation pierced what had up till now been commendable

60

DISCOVERY

patience. "You wouldn't have me turn
this opportunity down, surely? A cruise in the Greek
Isles, all found? It's extremely good of Sandra to invite us!"

"Us?" Richard's eyes bulged. "Who else is going?"

"Ellen. I thought I'd said." Jane's tone had resumed its former patient
note. "Things haven't been particularly good between her and Ted lately,
so it will give her a break, too."

"It's all right for her; she hasn't any children to consider," Richard said
heavily.

"That's true," Jane acknowledged.

And, if you weren't so obtuse, she added silently, you'd realise that
having no children can be a source of misery, rather than a source of relief!

61

He wasn't normally this insensitive, she knew. He was scared; just plain scared of coping on his own for eight days.

"You'll manage," she told him cheerfully. "Chloé will help you, won't you?"

She looked across at her eleven-year-old daughter, listening intently.

"Don't you worry, Mum, I'll take care of things," the girl said stoutly. She eyed her father reproachfully. "You ought to be glad Mum's getting the chance of a holiday like this, Dad," she told him.

"I am," Richard said hastily. "But I don't know about the three of you going alone. I mean, all those ship's officers, in their fancy uniforms."

"Yes," Jane murmured thoughtfully.

"There's a glint in your eyes I don't like the look of," Richard accused.

"So long as it remains just a glint, there's no need for you to worry, is there?" she rejoined sweetly. "Anyway, what would they want with an old married lady like me?"

"They're always nice to the women passengers; it's their job," Richard muttered.

"Thank *you!*" There was a wry note in Jane's voice. "If I see a handsome chap in a white-and-gold-uniform, smiling my way, I'll do well to remember that."

"Oh, Jane, you know I was only joking . . . You're only thirty-two and well . . . pretty attractive really . . ."

"Thank you again," she replied wryly. "I'll remember that, too, while I'm away."

"So you're going; leaving me to cope . . ."

"I'm going," Jane said gently.

It was nice, though, she reflected later, to feel she would be missed. She couldn't help wondering, a little sadly, if Ellen's husband, Ted, would react in the same way.

$$\star \quad \star \quad \star \quad \star$$

"It sounds a good idea." Ted looked up from the papers he was working on. "Things will be all right here. You go ahead and make your plans."

He returned to his work. Ellen eyed him silently. She wondered if he had even listened to what she was saying, or whether he would notice when she had gone. It hurt to think he wouldn't miss her yet she wasn't surprised.

Her sister's invitation had come out of the blue, and, suddenly, she welcomed the prospect of a breathing space, to sort out in her mind whether there was any chance — or indeed if she wanted one — of saving what was left of this marriage.

There hadn't been another woman for him — nor another man for her. The enemy was indifference — and it was winning the fight . . .

She wondered briefly if he would be here when she returned from the cruise — or whether she would return here herself.

They had already talked of a separation and she had intimated that she would be prepared to move back to her mother's and leave Ted the flat, until things were sorted out.

Eyeing her husband's head, bent over his work again, she had a feeling that was probably the best thing for them both . . .

The *Aphrodite* was sleek and luxurious and the weather glorious. For once they had time to plan what to wear to dinner, instead of what to cook. They could spend as long as they liked doing the things *they* wanted to do when *they* wanted to do them.

They loved trying new hair styles, like teenagers, and dressing for dinner and absolutely adored eating someone else's cooking, but they talked about home and their respective families much more than they'd thought they would.

In just a few days, Jane had colour in her cheeks, Sandra noted. And, as for Ellen, that air of tension that had been so noticeable at the start of the holiday had left her completely.

As for herself, she was relaxed and happy in the knowledge that Jack would cope admirably during her absence . . .

There's really nothing to all this, Jack was thinking, far away.

The automatic washing machine would take care of his laundry and the microwave was a godsend.

If the girls enjoyed themselves, he thought magnanimously as he pushed a frozen chicken dinner into the microwave, then wandered back to the living-room and switched on the television, there was no reason why they shouldn't have a little break like this every year . . .

He spared a moment's sympathy for his brother-in-law, Richard. It wouldn't be so easy for him — he was hopeless without Jane.

There were a lot of men like that around, he reflected, trying not to sound smug.

Smiling, he strolled into the kitchen to fill the washing machine . . .

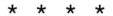

To his credit, Richard had managed the shopping — with a little help from Chloé. He had found trundling a trolley round the supermarket a harassing experience and had been amazed at the amount of money he seemed to have spent, when he got to the checkout.

Between them, he and Chloé put the groceries away.

"I think we deserve a cup of coffee after that, love," he called out to his daughter in the kitchen.

"Right. Coffee coming up!" Minutes later, she appeared in the doorway. "I thought you put some coffee in the trolley."

"Me?" Richard looked askance at her. "I distinctly saw *you* . . ." He sighed heavily. "Mum wouldn't have forgotten the coffee, would she?" he muttered at last. "And I need some clean shirts. When did she say she would be back?"

"Come on!" Chloé gave him an affectionate thump on the back. "You don't want her to think we can't manage without her, do you?"

"We can't," Richard said fervently. "And I'll make sure she knows that when she comes home —" He broke off as the telephone sounded.

Picking up the receiver, he heard his brother-in-law, Jack's, voice, its usual benevolent tone markedly absent . . .

THE flat was definitely quieter without Ellen, Ted thought, which was strange, considering the fact that they didn't talk much these days.

Throwing down his pen, he stood up and paced the room. This was what it would be like when she left. They had practically agreed she would do that, at some future point.

He was surprised how much the thought depressed him. They had been growing apart for some time now — she with her committees and he with his job.

She had gone back to work herself a year or two ago, once they had finally realised there would never be any children. Yet, instead of fulfilling her and making things better between them, the gulf had widened.

Things shouldn't have been allowed to get to this stage, he reflected, just because they had found it impossible to have a family.

The place depressed him suddenly and brought on a surprising feeling of loneliness.

He could go down to his local, yet none of his friends were there on Tuesday nights.

Sighing, he returned determinedly to the papers he had been working on. Yet, after a few minutes, he threw down his pen again and reached for the telephone.

On impulse, he dialled his brother-in-law's number.

"Oh, it's you, Ted." Richard sounded surprised. As well he might, Ted thought wryly, recalling how many years it was since he had last telephoned him.

"I just wondered if you'd heard from the girls," Ted murmured.

"The post takes time, coming from other countries," Richard pointed out. "I expect you're managing pretty well without Ellen."

"Oh, definitely!" Ted agreed quickly. "We've no children to worry about, of course . . ."

Somehow, it sounded like a plea for sympathy, which hadn't been his intention at all. He'd just thought he would call . . .

"You almost missed me; I was just on my way out," Richard told him.

"Oh, well, don't let me keep you —" Ted withdrew sharply.

"I was only going down to Jack's," Richard explained. "It'll keep a minute. He's having some kind of problem with his plumbing and I said I'd see what I could do.

"Maybe we could get together later . . . a drink or something . . ."

"Definitely." Ted hesitated, gripping the receiver tightly.

"Look, I'll come down to Jack's if you like. I might be able to help; you never know."

"Glad to have you aboard," Richard responded.

An unfortunate remark to make in the circumstances, he thought wryly, when all three of us have been abandoned for a boat out in the Aegean somewhere . . .

THE kitchen was ankle deep when Richard and Chloé arrived at Jack's. Jack himself was running around like a scalded hen, his usual serenity thrown to the winds.

"I only turned the washing machine on and look at this!" he wailed despairingly. "And, naturally, no plumber will turn out at this time of day. And messing about with this, I forgot the microwave and I've had a fire in it. And the television's packed up."

He ran a despairing hand through his hair.

Richard looked around. "I hope you're never asked to turn on the Christmas lights," he commented.

"Where's your water tap, for a start?"

They managed to get things under control, though the kitchen carpet was ruined, along with part of the dining-room carpet, where the water had seeped across.

Jack was frantic.

"I need to get a message to Sandra," he said distractedly. "She could get off the boat at one of their ports of call and fly back —"

"Oh, come on!" Richard exclaimed. Somehow, Jack's disaster, while eliciting his sympathy, had given his own self-esteem an enormous boost. All *he'd* done so far was forget the coffee . . .

"You surely don't want her thinking you can't manage without her?"

He caught Chloé's eye, then, and had the grace to look embarrassed.

The doorbell rang. Ted was standing on the threshold when Jack opened the door, his arms full of packages, from one of which, Richard saw with interest, protruded several bottles.

"I thought the best thing I could do to help was bring a take-away and a drink for when it's all over," Ted explained. "I'm hopeless on plumbing, anyway. How are things going?"

"Richard has everything under control," Jack told him.

Richard just smiled self-deprecatingly.

"You'd think we'd never been left on our own before, wouldn't you?" he murmured. "Do I smell a pizza, Ted?"

LATER, replete and full of bonhomie — Ted was particularly good at choosing wine — Richard sat back and regarded his brothers-in-law with a smile.

Strange, he thought. He'd known Ted for years, yet they'd never been close. Not that there was anything wrong with Ted but, with his high-powered job and living in a more upmarket area of town, they hadn't seemed to have much in common.

Yet, now, minus his jacket and with shirt sleeves rolled up as he fiddled with the stricken television set, he looked like one of them.

Yes, that was the best way to put it, Richard thought contentedly. Ted looked like one of the family, at last.

Ted's thoughts were busy, too. He had been part of this family for years, yet outside it. It wouldn't just be Ellen he lost, but the others too.

He'd never got to know Jack or Richard well, yet, at his loneliest point, he had turned to them and they hadn't let him down.

Was he prepared to lose all that by default? Because that's what it would be.

Ellen was slipping away from him, slowly yet surely, and he was allowing it to happen because it seemed easier.

This week, he'd had a foretaste of how it would be when the inevitable happened and Ellen left.

And it wasn't just that. Little things, like catching sight of her clothes in the wardrobe, or picking up mail addressed to her, made him realise just how intertwined their lives were and how awful it would be, when the break came.

Last night, lying wakeful in the darkness, he had tried to imagine life without her. And he hadn't been able to . . .

He'd had no right to risk all that, he realised now. They could make things work, they *could*. But it would need *both* of them to try.

No more hiding behind work for him, nor more throwing herself into her committee work for Ellen, in an effort to forget her pain.

Tuning the television set back on, he sat back to contemplate the far more important job of mending his marriage.

As for Jack, he just hoped and prayed that no more windfalls would come Sandra's way . . .

"I wish I could say I'm looking forward to going home," Sandra said lazily. "But I'm not. I could stay here in this deck-chair for ever."

"Me, too,' Jane murmured, from the adjoining chair. "I can't help worrying, though, about the state of things back home."

"Now, that's something I definitely am not thinking about." Sandra spoke contentedly. "Jack has no problem coping on his own!"

Listening, Ellen made no comment. The flat would be perfectly tidy, she thought, and Ted would be in his usual place, head bent over his work.

All three women closed their minds determinedly to the situation back home, and turned their faces towards the sun . . .

YET, all good things come to an end, and the time came for the sisters to leave the ship and fly home.

A smile broke over Sandra's face as she caught sight of her husband hovering anxiously in the crowd when they arrived.

"Hello, love. Good trip?" He smiled as the group reached him.

"Wonderful, love. Have things been all right?" Sandra asked, returning his kiss.

"Great!" And, if he spoke a little too heartily, Sandra didn't notice in her pleasure at seeing him. It was good to be home.

"In fact . . ." He cleared his throat. "I've bought you a present to welcome you back. Thought it was time we had a new microwave; we've had that one for years."

Ignoring her exclamation of delight, he hurried on. "And I got a new kitchen carpet, too. Thought I might as well go the whole hog, while I was at it. That washing-machine's on its last legs, too."

"Jack!" Sandra could hardly contain her happiness. "How on earth did you manage —?"

"Oh —" He touched his nose and smiled. "You're not the only one who has windfalls, love." He seemed anxious to change the subject.

"I've brought Richard and Chloé down with me," he said, looking at Jane. "They went for a newspaper."

Jane had already seen her husband and daughter approaching and was waving excitedly.

"Glad to be back?" Richard asked good-humouredly, as he reached her side. "You look well, anyway."

He studied her critically. "The trip's done you good. I was only saying to Jack on the way here that you ought to go more often.

"Chloé and I can cope well enough, can't we?" He looked down at his daughter without a trace of a blush.

"Piece of cake," Chloé agreed solemnly.

"Oh, Ellen, look!" Jane exclaimed, pointing to the entrance.

Her sister had already seen the man who had wandered into the airport lounge carrying the largest bunch of flowers she'd ever seen — but could hardly believe it was Ted.

Her heart was thumping madly as he approached, the uncertainty was written all over his face. And to think she'd been so worried at how much she'd missed *him.*

"Good trip?" Ted asked, as she reached his side.

"Wonderful," she told him. "I didn't expect —"

"I missed you, Ellen," he broke in simply, and handed her the flowers.

They stared at each other for a moment, then Ellen nodded. "I hoped you would," she said, almost shyly.

All in all, Sandra reflected, as the group made its way towards the car park, the cruise had done them good. All of them! ∎

68

Romance In The Air

by Valerie Cantrell

... there was also an unexpected announcement that would raise a few eyebrows ...

IT took Linda for ever to get ready. But then it always did, so Margaret was well used to entertaining her daughter's current beau whilst he waited, not always patiently, for Linda's transformation.

"She takes a long time, doesn't she?" Michael asked, his large, brown eyes leaving the tray of jam tarts Margaret had just taken from the oven only long enough to flick upwards at the kitchen clock.

"She certainly does," Margaret agreed. "Linda!" she called, stepping from the kitchen into the hall. "Do hurry up! Michael is waiting for you!"

"Nearly ready!" a distant, small voice answered. "Just doing my hair."

Margaret deftly removed the bubbling tarts from their tray and placed one of them on a small plate.

"That's for you," she told Michael with a smile, "but wait until it cools down a little."

"Thanks!" Michael grinned at her, a dark mahogany curl hanging over one eye.

He really is handsome, Margaret thought, as she bustled around the kitchen. Those liquid-brown eyes with their shading fans of long, dark lashes would melt the coldest heart.

And when he smiled! A deep dimple divided each cheek, heralding the appearance of dazzling white, even teeth and the smouldering eyes would sparkle with a mischievous light.

Margaret mentally admired her daughter's good taste.

A heartfelt "Oh, no!" made her turn from her baking.

Michael stood, arms outstretched, watching in dismay as a large blob of apricot jam slithered down the front of his black dinner jacket.

"Come over here," Margaret said with a smile, wiping her floury hands.

Gently, she sponged until the sticky mark disappeared,

69

hiding her amusement at Michael's embarrassed grin. She straightened his bow-tie.

"HELLO," came a shy voice from behind them. They turned quickly to face the figure in the doorway.

At a glance, Margaret realised that Linda's taste in clothes and make-up was nowhere near as good as her taste in males.

Her tanned complexion, a perfect foil for her cornblonde, long hair, had disappeared under a liberal layer of too-pale powder, and the orange lipstick was the last colour Margaret would have chosen to go with the cyclamen dress.

The sweep of green eyeshadow did emphasise the wide, forget-me-not eyes, but could have been applied just a little less generously, and a light brown eyebrow pencil would have flattered her fairness better than the brownish-black she had chosen.

A glimpse of black, high-heeled shoes with diamanté buckles could be seen at her hemline and two sparkling rings, a jewelled comb and a rhinestone-encrusted evening bag completed her ensemble.

With a sideways glance at Michael, whose expression, she noted, revealed nothing but admiration, Margaret tactfully decided to offer no criticism.

Michael, meanwhile, continued to stare.

"That's a nice dress," he said finally.

Linda rewarded him with a special smile.

"Let's go into the garden," she suggested.

Margaret made a pot of tea and stood at the sink to watch as the youngsters walked slowly in the warmth of the early-evening sunshine across the emerald grass.

STOPPING by a rose bush, Linda picked two blood-red buds and invited Michael to share their sweet scent. Smiling shyly, she fastened one in his buttonhole and secured the second in her hair beneath her jewelled comb.

As they walked on, Linda stumbled and Michael grasped her hand.

He didn't release it, Margaret noticed, even though Linda had regained her balance.

The rustic seat, set in a bower of pink roses, was spotlighted by the low, slanting sun rays, and flashes of light sparkled from Linda's hair, fingers and feet as the young couple sat down.

For a moment, neither spoke, then, not meeting Linda's eyes, Michael said quietly, "I think I'd like to marry you."

"I'd like to marry you, too, Michael," Linda whispered.

So absorbed was Margaret in her daughter's developing romance that she didn't hear her husband's slippered footsteps. The soft touch of his hands on her hips and the gentle kiss beneath her right ear startled her slightly.

"Look at them, Bob," she murmured. "Don't they make a lovely couple?"

With his face against his wife's and his arms around her, Bob stayed to watch the love scene unfolding in their sunlit garden.

"Do you think we're losing our daughter to that handsome brute?" he murmured in Margaret's ear.

"It certainly looks that way," she agreed quietly. "He's quite a hunk, isn't he?"

They parted reluctantly as Michael and Linda neared the open kitchen door.

"We're going to get married," Linda announced with a radiant smile, first at Michael and then at her parents.

Margaret and Bob exchanged a quick glance. Bob recovered first.

"Congratulations, old man!" He shook hands with Michael.

Margaret kissed them both. "I hope you'll both be very happy — I couldn't have wished for a nicer son-in-law!"

Michael grinned sheepishly.

"I'm going to have a baby," Linda announced as she climbed on to a tall, kitchen stool.

Her high heels dropped to the floor with a clatter.

Her parents fought to control their expressions.

"When?" Michael asked, with only mild surprise. "Please may I have another jam tart?"

"Soon," Linda answered.

Bob bent and lifted Michael on to a stool. Below the dinner jacket, his thin brown legs and flip-flops swung contentedly and the bow-tie bobbed against his bare neck as he swallowed.

He brushed crumbs from the front of his "Superman" T-shirt, and Linda wiped her mouth with the back of her hand, leaving a smear of orange lipstick almost to her ears. The children giggled.

MARGARET placed a glass of milk in front of each of them and put an arm around each small body.

"Finish your milk and then go and put the dressing-up things away," she told them with a hug. "It's nearly time for Michael to go home."

As the children scampered away, Bob and Margaret collapsed into each other's arms.

"Men!" Margaret chuckled. "All he thought of when she dropped her bombshell was his stomach.

"Women!" Bob laughed softly as he kissed the top of his wife's nose. "She might have told the poor chap it was a baby brother or sister she was going to have!"

He held Margaret as close as her advanced pregnancy would allow and kissed her again.

Then, still laughing, and with an arm around each other, they walked down the hall to supervise the children's re-appearance as five-year-olds. ∎

BARNEY'S

I knew the children would mourn the passing of their beloved pet. It was the reaction of her doggy pal which came as such a surprise...

BEST FRIEND

by Teresa Ashby

I WALKED woodenly from the room, carefully measuring every step. I did not look back. I had a very important duty to perform.

In the kitchen, Barney looked up from his bed, his tail wagging gently, but not in joy.

"I'm sorry, Barney," I said, kneeling down in front of him. "Honey's gone. There was nothing Tim could do for her this time."

Barney looked at me with his huge, liquid, seal-brown eyes. He knew, oh, he knew.

The door opened and closed softly behind me and I turned to see Tim standing there.

His untidy, greying hair usually reminded me of a mad professor rather than a vet, but today I was in no mood for such comparisons.

"Have you told him?" he asked.

I nodded, the lump in my throat not allowing me to speak. Then I smiled, a strange, wobbly kind of smile.

This was insane, wasn't it? Telling a dog, as if he understood, that his best friend had just died — and with the full backing of the vet!

Tim placed his hand gently on my shoulder.

"Would you like me to talk to the children when they get home?"

"No, thanks, Tim." I found my voice. "I'll do it."

"I'll leave you to it, then," Tim replied, embarrassed. "If you need me at all . . ." His voice tailed away.

"I've got your number," I said.

When he'd gone, shutting the door behind him, the floodgates opened and I gave full and final vent to my grief.

I felt as if I were being torn apart from the inside out. I didn't know such pain existed, but when it was over, I knew I'd be better for it.

Barney lay on his bed, his white muzzle resting on his huge paws, staring at Honey's empty cushion.

I would have to remove it, of course, and any other poignant reminders of Honey.

As I reached for the cushion, Barney got up, ambled forward, picked it up and carried it back to his own bed, his head high in a vain attempt to keep it clear of the floor.

Then he lay down again, his chin resting on the cushion, challenging me to take it away.

"She's dead, Barney," I said firmly. But I allowed him to keep the cushion anyway.

Five years ago, Barney had come into our lives, a seven-week-old Retriever pup with big, floppy, golden-coloured ears and feet like dinner plates. He fitted so naturally into our lives and we all fell in love with him from the word go.

My husband had recently left us, taking his six-year-old border collie, Honey, with him.

It was the most heartless, cruel thing he could have done and Barney was my way of making up the loss of Honey to the children.

I wasn't to know that Malcolm would take a job on an oil rig within three months and bring Honey back to us. Not that it mattered. Honey adored the pup and mothered him right from the start, even though he soon grew to be much bigger than her.

There was no need to train Barney to come back to us, as Honey would always decide when he should return and go after him, rounding him up and heading him back.

She took on a new lease of life and, somehow, Barney made up for all the weeks of upheaval she'd had to endure.

There were rules, though. Honey had her cushion and guarded it jealously, never allowing Barney anywhere near it.

If there were table scraps going, then Honey took her place at the head of the queue and Barney would sit back and wait until it was his turn when he would wolf down his share greedily.

And when Honey got herself into a fight, Barney ploughed in to rescue her, earning himself a torn ear which he carried with immense pride.

They were truly inseparable. I saw my solicitor and had it written into the divorce papers that Honey stayed with us permanently.

And now she'd gone . . .

I sighed and stood up to switch on the kettle. Soon Katy and Sam would be back from school and I'd have to break the news to them.

I had the tea ready when they came in, squabbling as usual over something trivial.

"Hey!" Sam got straight on to his knees. "What's up with Barney? Why hasn't he come to say 'hello'?"

"Oh, Mum," Katy gripped the edge of the kitchen dresser, her face going

74

pale. "It's Honey, isn't it? What happened? Is she very ill?"

Sam was still on his knees. He was looking at Honey's cushion, which Barney still hugged.

"She's dead, isn't she?" he said.

I could never have known how Honey's death would affect us all.

SAM was 13 years old, but every night his pillow was wet. He was just a toddler when we got Honey and couldn't remember a time when she wasn't there.

Katy was 15. She didn't cry, but held her grief inside.

As for me, I couldn't have imagined the gaping emptiness Honey's passing would leave within me.

But it was Barney who was really heartbroken.

He didn't bolt his food with his usual enthusiasm. He stopped cadging at the table and even chocolate and cheese and other treats failed to bring that old smile to his eyes.

"He's getting so thin, Mum." Katy pointed out to me one day when he turned down the offer of a prawn cocktail crisp — always his favourite after-dinner snack.

I ran my hand along his back. She was right. His bones were poking through his flesh and lumps had appeared along his back.

"I'll see Tim," I murmured, and Sam glared at me accusingly.

"No," he said.

"It wasn't Tim's fault that Honey had to die," I said. "He simply ended her pain. If there was anything that could have been done, don't you think he would have tried?"

Barney began to rub the lumps on his back by standing underneath the dining-table.

It was quite amusing at first to see the table moving about the room — until we noticed the raw patches he was rubbing in his skin.

"He's pining," Tim declared after examining him. "There's certainly no sign of disease or illness."

"What about his back?"

"That's all part of it," he said. "I can treat it, but . . ."

"But?" My eyes glittered, I willed him to offer me anything but the alternative I did not want.

"But, it will go on getting worse until, well, until he stops missing Honey."

"He'll never stop missing her," I said, finally accepting that terrible fact.

"This is a long shot . . . it may not work — in fact, it could have the opposite effect, but . . . a puppy might be the answer," Tim said.

"Are you mad?"

"No, just slightly insane." He grinned, his brown eyes kind as always.

"I — I don't know. I'd have to think about it, talk it over with the kids . . ."

"Don't leave it too long." He touched Barney's bony body, a note of warning in his voice. "Fred Anderson at Hill Farm has some collie pups."

"I said I'll think about it," I replied, hurrying out of the surgery, trying to ignore the sympathetic glances of those waiting.

Poor Barney. He looked ragged and sick and I knew he couldn't go on like this for much longer.

FRED ANDERSON was a huge man with powerful arms and a shock of auburn hair. He was shy, not given to idle conversation, but the sight of poor Barney was enough to drive his embarrassment away.

I knew his dogs were good. Our Honey had been one of his.

He took us round the back of the farmhouse to the outdoor pen where he kept the pups.

"I'll let them out," he said to me, then looking at Barney, shook his head sadly. I knew he thought it was hopeless, but I had to try.

Six rolling, tumbling black and white bodies fell out of the pen and raced across the grass. They were beautiful, each and every one of them.

Barney stood stock still as they cautiously approached him. Their mother stood close by. Somehow she knew Barney wouldn't harm her offspring.

He didn't so much as lower his head to sniff the pups.

I tried to interest him in them, he stood rigid, staring straight ahead.

Sam and Katy were not so strong. Both were on their knees with the pups. Sam looked at me with eyes that said, "Please, Mum."

"OK," I sighed. "But if Barney doesn't get along with the pup . . ."

I hate to admit it and I hated myself for thinking it, but at the back of my mind was the thought that a puppy would help soften the blow when Barney himself eventually died.

Fred shook his head and tugged at his chin.

"I can always take the pup back," he muttered. "There's never any shortage of takers for my dogs."

"Which one is it to be, then?" I asked, but I needn't have bothered. He'd already been chosen. A robust dog with a black face and a white blaze on his chest.

He was sitting, leaning against Sam's leg and offering Katy his paw.

"Can I call back in a couple of days for him, Fred?" I asked, and as always, the big farmer was willing to oblige.

I watched sadly as he put the pups back in their pen and took a last, lingering look at their feathery ears before turning to go.

Barney looked at me, hurt in his eyes. I felt guilty for attempting to replace Honey, but I was desperate and time, for Barney, was running out.

FRED walked with us back to the car and as we passed his front porch, a golden streak shot out of nowhere, right across our path.

Barney actually noticed something.

His head flicked to one side and he watched in fascination as the ginger kitten tore about the yard.

Fred swore under his breath and gave chase, but the kitten dodged and darted just out of his reach until at last he noticed Barney.

He stopped still and stared at the flop-eared dog.

Fred could easily have caught him then, but there was something in Barney's eyes that stopped him, a light which had been missing for too long.

I didn't dare breathe as the kitten turned sideways on and began to half hop towards Barney.

Suddenly, the lead jerked and Barney was half lying down, his front end on the ground, his rear end in the air and wagging like mad.

He took a little leap towards the kitten and assumed the same posture.

Fred looked at me. I looked at him. Barney hated cats. Ever since the Siamese from across the road had scratched his nose, making it bleed when he was young.

The kitten, unafraid of the dog, kept on coming, keeping to his sideways stance so that he was ready to run, if necessary.

It seemed to go on for ever. The kitten edging closer, Barney waiting.

The thought crossed my mind briefly, what if Barney pounces on the kitten and hurts it?

I tightened my hold on his lead, just in case.

The kitten came closer. Barney slowly, gently, lowered his bottom so that he was lying flat on the ground, panting now. He lay still as the kitten completed his approach.

Miraculously, they rubbed noses and the kitten began to purr loudly, the noise the only sound in that quiet farmyard.

Barney lay, gentle as a lamb, while the kitten explored him, climbed over his back, nibbled his ears, patted his nose with tiny paws.

"Take him home with you," Fred said gruffly. "It's the last of a litter. I was going to keep him, but the little beggar's more trouble than he's worth."

"Oh, I couldn't do that," I began.

Fred laughed, a jolly, hearty sound which was a rare treat. "I don't think you have any choice, my dear!"

"Can we still have the puppy?" Sam asked as Katy quickly scooped the kitten into her arms.

"I don't see why not," I said. I was so pleased that Barney was happy that I think I'd have agreed to anything!

And now, a year on, I know I made the right decision — or rather Barney did.

Sam and Shad the collie are inseparable, real friends, the way a boy and his dog should be. Barney curls up contentedly with Duke the cat — on the end of Katy's bed when I'm not looking!

And me? With all these young pets, I'm getting to know a certain vet with bushy, greying hair and gentle brown eyes a whole lot better! ■

A wedding
in the family!
We were all
delighted —
and dying to
know who would
be giving the
bride away . . .

by Teresa Ashby

Chrissie's Choice

I SANK down on the stairs, my hands shaking as I re-read those words a few more times just to be sure.

. . . and so Jack and I have decided to get married in March, in the old church of St Mary's.

I know you'll be happy for us, Mum, and . . .

Chrissie, married . . . at last!

"Oh!" I gasped. "Oh, my goodness!"

Married in March — that didn't give me very long to arrange things — supposing she *did* want me to arrange things, that is.

Quickly, I skimmed through the letter again . . . Yes, she *had* definitely asked me to set the wheels in motion.

"What is it, love?" Ray came downstairs, rubbing his hair with a towel. "Not bad news?" He came to me, concern written all over his face.

"On the contrary." I grinned up at my husband. "It's from Chrissie . . . and she's getting married!" I felt so excited.

"Oh, darling, I *am* pleased." Ray sat down beside me on the stairs and gave me a congratulatory hug.

"She wants me to arrange everything," I went on proudly.

"She's getting married here then?" He looked as delighted as I felt. "At St Mary's?"

"In March — right at the start, I think. I suppose she wants to be like . . . her father and me."

"That's only natural." Ray gave me another understanding hug.

John, my first husband, and I had been married at St Mary's in March.

He had died suddenly and tragically from a cerebral haemorrhage when he was only 30 and so it had been a real struggle bringing Chrissie up on my own — but I was so glad I'd had her, I'd kept reminding myself.

All through those difficult years, caring for her had helped me cope with my own grief.

Through Chrissie, I'd had this constant contact with John. His memory was always alive for me whenever I looked at my daughter.

And so I hadn't felt any real bitterness about being left with a child to bring up, only a lingering sadness about John's premature death.

My own dad, a widower himself, had been a tower of strength all these years and John's folk had always taken a great interest in Chrissie. With John being an only child, she was their last link with the son they'd lost.

When John's mother had died a few years ago, his father, Ted, had become even more a part of our family.

And the way things have worked out now — marrying Ray and now Chrissie getting married — I really couldn't be happier . . .

At the time, I'd devoted myself to bringing up my daughter, but once she'd left home to go to university, I began to think more of taking stock of my own life, and that's how I'd come to enrol in a drama class.

Once I'd started, I'd found myself falling hopelessly in love with the teacher, who just happened to be Ray!

Around the same time, Chrissie, too, had fallen hopelessly in love with a fellow student called Jack. He's a tall, thin lad with a mop of fair, spiky hair and ice-cool blue eyes, which don't match his warm personality.

"She'll want someone to give her away, of course." Ray beamed at me, interrupting my dreaming.

"Yes," I said thoughtfully. "I suppose she will."

"Does she mention any names in her letter?"

I shook my head. There was a list of bridesmaids, ushers, even the best man, but no mention of who was to give her away.

Ray took the towel off his head and draped it round his neck. I could tell by the look on his face that he expected to be asked.

"Do you suppose . . .?" he began, but I was saved by the oven timer buzzing furiously.

I made my escape to the kitchen and busied myself with a batch of apple pies for the freezer.

Apart from the problem of who was to give her away, I was thrilled to bits. Chrissie and Jack had been living together for five years now and I was beginning to think they'd never get round to marriage.

"There's no hurry, Mum," Chrissie would say if I tentatively dropped heavy hints. "We're still at university. There'll be plenty of time for getting married later on . . . maybe when we want kids," she'd added tauntingly.

"Well —" I'd bluster "— I didn't mean to poke my nose in or anything . . ."

"Of course you didn't!" She'd drop a kiss on my forehead, making me feel like the younger, less-experienced person.

She was so like John, too — attractive and tall — and she'd shot past me, in height, by the time she was twelve.

Then when they'd left university, they'd both been lucky to obtain good, well-paid jobs, but still there was no real indication that they were thinking of marriage.

"Don't fret, Mum, we'll get round to it, one of these days," Chrissie assured me breezily.

"We're both busy career building at the moment. We simply haven't the time . . ."

And so it went on. Until now.

THE next time Ray tried to broach the subject, the telephone rang — and saved me again.

"Hello, love." It was my dad, and from the cheerful tone of his voice, it was quite obvious that he'd heard from Chrissie, too.

I wondered if . . .

"So, she's making an honest man of him at last." Dad was prattling on. "She doesn't mention in her letter who'll be giving her away. I don't suppose you . . .?"

"She hasn't told me either, Dad," I intervened apologetically.

"Well, she can hardly ask Ted with his gammy leg and Ray, well, much as I like Ray, you've only been married five minutes and . . ."

"Four *years*, Dad!" I sighed.

"Pardon? What did you say?"

"I've been married to Ray for four years."

"Yes, but, he wasn't there to see Chrissie grow up like I was," Dad protested.

"I'm sure Chrissie will make the right decision," I assured him, ringing off.

Turning to look at Ray, I noticed he was looking a little peeved.

"That was your dad, wasn't it?" he said. "He thinks *he* should give her away."

"Ray, I . . ."

"There's no need to explain." Ray put up both his hands and smiled in mock admission of defeat, but he couldn't fool me. He couldn't hide the hurt he was feeling.

He'd grown very fond of Chrissie over the past few years, but the fact remained that no-one seemed to have a clear right to give my daughter away.

"Trouble is," Ray added, "what on earth are you going to tell Ted?"

AS if on cue, Ted's face appeared at the kitchen window. He waved and I went to open the door.

"I've had a letter from Chrissie," he told me excitedly, waving the sheet of notepaper under my nose. "She's getting married."

"That's right, Ted," I said, "would you like some tea?"

I couldn't help wondering if, in the letter, Chrissie had asked Ted to give her away. After all, he was her father's father and consequently, he probably had the strongest claim on the much-sought-after honour.

He settled himself at the kitchen table, and exchanged a few words with Ray about the rights and wrongs of taking fuchsia cuttings in the winter.

Ray, bless his heart, who wouldn't know a fuchsia if it walked up to him and introduced itself, sat listening attentively, as if taking it all in.

Perhaps he was.

Perhaps Ted would make a gardener of him yet!

"You see, your hardwood cuttings will root quickly in a glass of water and by the time the frost's clear, you've got some sturdy, well-established plants."

Ray nodded, his forehead creasing in concentration.

"Now, your softwood cuttings . . ."

I PLACED a steaming mug of tea in front of my father-in-law and something — perhaps the homely kitchen scene — reminded me of my brother, Malcolm.

He was still in his teens when John died, but he'd been wonderful — doing all the things with Chrissie that a father would do with his child. He'd taken her boating on the lake, exploring in the woods, searching along leafy lanes for the biggest conkers — all these things and more.

★ ★ ★ ★

"No," I heard Ray say distantly. "No, she hasn't said a word about it to us, has she, Sylvie?"

"About what?"

But before they told me, I sensed exactly what they were talking about.

"I know I've got this gammy leg," Ted muttered, tapping his calf with his walking stick, "but I won't let the girl down.

"As John's father, I think it's only right and proper that I should be the one to give her away formally."

I bit my lip and looked at Ray. He was looking quite smug. As far as he was concerned, he was the only possible choice in the "giving away" stakes.

This was because, if Chrissie were to choose between her grandfathers, it would be sure to hurt, irrevocably, the feelings of the one who was rejected. And she wouldn't want to do that if she could possibly avoid it.

However, it obviously hadn't occurred to any of them that my brother might be another strong contender.

There was only one thing for it as far as I could see, to ask Chrissie straight out, and put them all out of their misery.

So that evening, I rang her.

"I haven't made up my mind yet," she told me, mysteriously, over the phone.

"Why, is there a problem?"

"You could say that," I replied. "So far there are three willing volunteers champing at the bit and I expect Malcolm to join them very shortly."

"Uncle Malcolm?" she sounded worried. "I hadn't even considered *him*! I suppose I should, though, shouldn't I?"

"It's up to you," I said.

"And I thought it was all going to be so straightforward," she said.

"You're not thinking of calling it off, are you?" I blurted out before I could stop myself.

"Certainly not!" she laughed. "It's taken us long enough to get round to it, if we call it off now, we might never get married."

I covered the mouthpiece so that she wouldn't hear my long sigh of relief.

"Tell you what," she continued happily. "Jack and I were thinking of driving down to see you all at the weekend. I'll have made up my mind by then. Do you think they'll be able to wait that long?"

"They'll just have to," I told her. "It won't do them any harm to stew for a bit longer, but, Chrissie . . ."

"I know," she said. "Look, don't worry, Mum, I promise I won't hurt anyone's feelings. Perhaps they could all come for lunch or something?"

She sounded so sure about it all, but did she truly appreciate the delicacy of the situation?

Anyway, it seemed a good idea to invite them all for Sunday lunch — it would get it all over with.

Chrissie and Jack arrived at midday on the Saturday, but Chrissie still refused to divulge the name of the favoured person.

It was beginning to sound like a lottery. I wondered if she intended to put all the names in a hat and draw out the lucky winner . . .

ARE you sure no-one's going to be hurt?" I asked her on the Sunday morning as she mixed the Yorkshire puddings for me.

"Positive," she said, smiling somewhat slyly, I thought, at Jack who, like Ray, was sitting reading the Sunday papers. "Trust me, Mother."

"I know," I said, "you've asked one of those weirdos from your college days . . ."

"Weirdos?" Chrissie burst out laughing.

"Honestly, Mum, I only met one weirdo and I'm marrying him!"

"I heard that," Jack mumbled from behind the paper.

"Why don't you two gentlemen go down to the pub for a drink before lunch? You're only getting in the way," I said, certain that once I had Chrissie on her own, she'd spill the beans.

After all, there was family loyalty to consider here. I had to be forewarned so that I knew whom I'd be comforting and sympathising with after lunch.

"Have I time for a quick shower?" Chrissie asked as soon as they'd gone.

"Yes, but . . ."

"Won't be long then, Mum." She grinned and disappeared upstairs.

She was still there when Malcolm and Julia arrived.

"Ram and Duck?" my brother queried when he saw the discarded newspapers.

"Black Horse."

"See you later, then."

"Nice to see you, too!" I shouted after him as he disappeared out of the door.

"Malcolm's only trying to get out of laying the table," Julia laughed.

She rummaged in the top drawer of the sideboard for table mats and cutlery and began to set the table.

"How many for lunch?"

"Eight, I think." I did a quick mental calculation. "Yes, eight."

"I take it the happy couple have arrived?" Julia enquired as she counted out the knives.

"Chrissie's in the shower, and Jack's . . ."

"At the Black Horse. Actually, I'm glad to have this chance to talk to you alone, Sylvie," Julia confided.

"We had a letter from Chrissie telling us about the wedding, but she didn't say anything about who was giving her away —"

"She hasn't told me either," I had to admit. "That's what today is all about. She'd going to make an announcement."

"An announcement?" Julia raised her eyebrows as she took the wine glasses from the cabinet and began setting them out. "But it's sure to be Malcolm . . . isn't it?" she added, suddenly uncertain.

"To tell you the truth, Julia, I have no idea," I confessed.

"Well, Malcolm has his heart set on giving Chrissie away," she said. "He'd never say so, of course, but I caught him trying on his best suit the other day . . ."

"Oh dear. Chrissie will do the right thing, I'm sure," I said brightly, trying to convince myself as well as Julia.

OVER lunch, no-one mentioned the wedding, probably because they were all too scared to bring up the one burning issue that was on all our minds.

I suppose if I had a favourite for the rôle of "giver away", it had to be Ray, but only because I loved him so much that I couldn't bear to see him hurt.

He kept glancing across at me and smiling hopefully.

Ted kept whacking his bad leg with his stick and saying, "The leg's a lot better these days, you know!"

And poor Dad kept reminiscing . . .

"Remember that day we spent in London, Chrissie? We went to Madam Tussaud's first and then to the Planetarium. You loved it there, and then . . ."

And Chrissie, like the dutiful, loving granddaughter she was, remembered.

"I bet you've forgotten when I took you on holiday to Devon and we went on the steam railway," Malcolm chimed in, attempting to make a case for himself.

"We stayed on a farm, remember, in a caravan and the farmer let you watch the cows being milked."

"I haven't forgotten, Uncle Malcolm," Chrissie said, her voice tinged with a little sadness, so that I knew Malcolm was not her choice. "It was the best holiday ever," she added tactfully.

Ray had nothing like that from the past to draw on. I could sense him desperately trying to think of something, though.

Julia cast worried glances at me and I prayed silently that soon Chrissie would put them all out of their misery.

"Ah!" Ray's face lit up as inspiration struck. "Talking of bridesmaids . . ."

"We weren't," Ted snapped uncharacteristically.

"Oh, well, I — I was just remembering what a lovely bridesmaid Chrissie was on *our* wedding day, Sylvie. It hardly seems possible that she's about to be a bride herself!"

A t last the meal was over, the dishes were piled up in the sink and we were finishing off with a cup of coffee.

A strained silence had descended upon the gathering. I looked over at my daughter. It was time.

"I haven't told you yet who I'm going to ask to give me away," she began, looking at each of the men in turn. "I've thought a lot about this, but in the end it was an easy decision to make." She smiled knowingly at us all.

"I decided there could really only be one person."

I glanced round the table noting how each male was thinking, confidently, that he was the chosen one.

Chrissie continued.

"I don't remember my dad properly, but I don't think I ever really suffered because of that.

"In fact, I think I did pretty well as a child. I had lots of extra attention.

"You, Gramps, often used to read me a story at bedtime and set me on course for sweet dreams. Do you remember?"

Ted positively swelled with pride.

"I remember, sweetheart." Ted smiled.

"And you, Grandad, had that special, little seat fitted to your bike so that you could take me all over the place with you. I loved that."

My dad smiled and for a moment, I could almost see them wobbling off down the road, Chrissie hanging on to her hat with one hand and the back of Dad's jacket with the other, totally confident in him.

"Uncle Malcolm —" she turned and reached across the table to touch his hand fondly "— you used to make me laugh! That's what I remember you for — the laughter. I could never be sad when I was with you."

86

Malcolm didn't say a word. He was too choked.

"And then, of course, there's Ray, who has made Mum so very happy." She looked across at Ray, her face showing her love for him.

"When you two got married, it was a dream come true for me. My dearest wish was to see you really happy again, Mum."

My eyes filled up and threatened to brim over at this point.

They were all on tenterhooks, all ready to shout out, "Get on with it! Who's it to be?"

But they didn't. They waited patiently as Chrissie continued, tears in *her* eyes by now.

"So you see, although my decision was an easy one in the long run, it wasn't made without some soul-searching. It had to be the person who was always there for me . . ."

She paused for a moment then she made the announcement we had all been waiting for. It was a shock to us all . . .

THERE was a numbing silence. Ted's mouth dropped open, Dad's cheeks turned bright pink and Malcolm looked for all the world like a boy who'd just had his ice-cream pinched.

I looked, in my confusion, at Ray. His face broke into a smile, then his shoulders began to shake. It wasn't long before everyone around the table was joining in and laughing heartily, releasing all the tension of the past week.

"You were right," Julia whispered in my ear. "She *has* done the right thing."

And as I looked round at the happy faces, I knew she really had.

Everyone was delighted with her choice.

And no-one was more pleased than I was.

"The Wedding March" boomed joyfully from the organ, the church doors were flung back and sunlight streamed in from outside as my daughter took her first step into the church.

Behind her, six pretty bridesmaids in white dresses bedecked with pink ribbons held their posies and white hymn books carefully.

At the altar, Jack waited patiently, his unruly hair brushed down. I saw him fidget nervously and my heart went out to him.

The long, long walk ended and all was still. I smiled about me at my father, at Ted, at Malcolm and lastly, and more lingeringly, at my dear Ray.

My throat ached as the service began. This was the proudest moment of my life.

At last the vicar asked, "Who gives this woman?"

I stepped forward, took a deep breath and said, "I do." ■

MEMORIES

My desk is above the city street.
I hear the tramp of a thousand feet.
I see the pallor of sunstarved faces.
The traffic roars and the busy clock races.

The telephone bell is forever ringing.
But in the depths of my mind the birds are singing.
There's a secret place where rabbits play
Where I can hide in my thoughts on a crowded day.

There, long ago, in my childhood days
I knew only the country ways.
Autumn wind in my hair, or a warm summer breeze.
The springtime beauty of new leafed trees.

I never thought then that my life would pass
In a concrete jungle devoid of grass.
But 'mid the typewriters' clack and the city gloom
I can leave in a flash that crowded room
And stand by the trees and watch rabbits at play
And my thoughts bring peace to my toilworn day.

Joyce Stranger

Inspired by an illustration by Mark Viney

A Room Full Of Memories

by Elizabeth Farrant

She'd been locked up in it – until a stranger provided the key to a brighter future.

THE back bedroom had always been Jenny's room, right from when she was a baby. Her bed had been in the corner when she was very small, but later they'd moved it nearer to the window.

The room overlooked the garden, and so, early on a summer morning, there was much to see: a blackbird tugging at a long juicy worm, a couple of bright-eyed blue-tits, once there had even been a shy grey squirrel — just a few feet from the window.

Jenny had always said how much she loved her bedroom . . .

The room had played a big part in Jenny's small, bright world — the world of a seven-year-old — busy, eventful, never a dull moment. The white shelves were covered with personal treasures — conkers and acorn-cups, her shell collection, the necklace that she'd made from melon pips. The bottom shelf held her pony annuals, her ballet shoes, her paint-box, her recorder . . .

Nothing had been moved or removed; nothing had changed. Except, that Jenny was no longer there.

Yvonne was standing beside the bedside table. Gently she gathered up a square of brightly-coloured knitting, still hanging heavy on its stout brown pins. It was part of the blanket Jenny had been making — the blanket which had been meant for her baby sister, Jilly's, cot.

Yvonne pressed it against her cheek until she could feel the large, uneven stitches.

When Yvonne was first expecting Jilly, she'd been slightly apprehensive that Jenny might be jealous of the baby.

Experienced friends with children were quick to warn her against all kinds of problems, and Yvonne had listened, hoping that none of these problems would apply to Jenny. After all, she was having this baby mainly for Jenny's sake.

Yvonne had always felt theirs was a perfect threesome — Bob, herself and Jenny. They'd had a lot of fun together as a family and she'd have been quite content for things to stay as they were.

Jenny was a happy, carefree child — friendly and sociable. But, not unnaturally, Yvonne had still been a little anxious when her only child had started school. She needn't have worried. Jenny, blithely, took it all in her stride.

In no time at all she'd made lots of new friends.

But not many of her friends were "only" children. Jenny came in from play one evening, and said thoughtfully, "I wish I had a baby sister. Twins would be best but one would do."

Yvonne and Bob had exchanged intimate glances. "We'll see, love," Yvonne had told her. "Maybe one day . . ."

And then, a year later there came the proud announcement in the local paper. *Madison — To Yvonne and Bob — a daughter, a sister for Jenny . . .* Yvonne still kept the cutting in her drawer.

Jenny had gone to school that day, triumphant. Over the previous months her excitement and anticipation of the coming event had been evident from the special entries in her news jotter. *It's only one week until my baby is born . . . my mummy is very fat now . . . it's only two days until my baby comes . . .*

She hadn't shown the slightest trace of jealousy. All she could think of was her gift for Jilly — six large, loosely-knitted squares in rainbow-coloured wools.

By the time Yvonne was home from hospital, the blanket was almost complete.

She remembered that mild September evening when she'd been sitting in the kitchen, feeding Jilly, while Jenny sat in a basket chair in the open doorway, knitting away in rapt concentration. She remembered the scene always in the sharpest detail.

"I'm on my last square now," Jenny had said. "Maybe I'll finish it before tomorrow."

"That'll be lovely, darling," Yvonne had murmured dreamily, lulled by the closeness and the warmth of baby Jilly.

"Perhaps I'll get it finished by tea-time, even."

"Lovely," Yvonne repeated. She held the baby up against her shoulder.

Thinking of tea-time had reminded her that she'd meant to buy some sausages that morning but with so much to do, she'd completely forgotten.

It had seemed quite natural to ask Jenny to go down to the friendly village shops, where the shopkeepers all knew her so well.

"Run along to the butcher's, darling, and get some of those nice sausages for tea . . ."

Jenny ran off happily into the September sunshine.

The house had seemed strangely quiet after she'd gone. Yvonne had sat peacefully holding the drowsy baby; warm, pleasant thoughts were drifting through her mind. At last, reluctantly, she roused herself. Time to put Jilly in her cot. Then she would scrub some potatoes. Jenny would soon be back . . . she was taking a while . . .

But when at last the doorbell rang, it wasn't Jenny standing on the step.

It was a dream . . . of course it was a dream. The baby in her arms was part of it . . . so was the patch of sunlight on the carpet . . . and Jenny's satchel, slung carelessly across the banister . . .

The policeman was young . . . he'd found it difficult to meet her eyes. "*There's been . . . an accident . . .*" he'd started to say. "*Your little girl . . .*"

TODAY was Saturday, and Bob was in the garden, spraying the roses. He turned his head and caught sight of her at the window. Once he'd have winked at her, his big, broad, friendly grin creasing his cheeks. Now he looked drawn and strained, his blue eyes anxious. He didn't like seeing her in Jenny's room because he knew it distressed her; brought back all the old memories.

"Vonny, let's clear her things away," he'd begged her gently, time and time again. "It only upsets you more, keeping the room like this. It can't bring Jenny back, love."

But that, Yvonne thought, was just where Bob was wrong. Among those small, familiar belongings, she felt quite close to Jenny. It helped to ease the pain a little. It did bring Jenny back to her, but not only Jenny, it brought back all those golden, tranquil days last summer — days when her world had seemed so safe, so happy and so perfect.

A light tap at the front door broke into her thoughts. Listlessly, Yvonne went to answer it.

The small, bright, bird-like woman standing on her doorstep might just as easily have come from another planet, as she beamed at Yvonne in greeting.

"I think you must be Mrs Madison . . . Forgive me — I know I'm being a nuisance, disturbing you on a Saturday afternoon, but I'm your new neighbour — Margaret Hathaway's the name."

The bird-like woman prattled on.

"I moved in yesterday — and, of course, I forgot to order any milk. So I wondered if, perhaps you . . ."

The tiny woman paused to take a breath.

It was a long time now, Yvonne was thinking, since anyone had smiled at her like this — cheerful, at ease, brimming with ordinary, carefree chatter.

Friends in the village who used to talk so freely when Jenny skipped along beside the pram, now greeted her cautiously, their smiles subdued or embarrassed.

Her new neighbour's face lit up again as she remembered something. "I've just been talking to your charming little girl."

Startled, Yvonne could only stare at first. Then, pulling herself together with an effort, she said quickly — "Oh, you mean Jilly?"

"Jilly. How sweet! The name suits her perfectly. So she's — not your only child?"

"Yes — she's my only one." Yvonne spoke briefly, conscious of a sharpness in her voice. "Come in, Mrs Hathaway. I'll get you some milk."

But the curtness was lost on Mrs Hathaway as she trotted happily behind Yvonne, glancing around the hall with obvious approval, and chattering all the time . . .

"A lovely home — and such a beautiful baby daughter! You must be so proud of her . . . sitting there so contented in her pram . . . and she's at such an interesting age . . .

"Oh, but I'm sure I'm hindering you, my dear. My husband — he passed away three years ago — he always used to tell me I talked too much. But, I simply can't resist children . . .

"We had no family of our own, you see, and I longed so much to have a little girl of my own . . . Ah, well," she sighed. "It wasn't to be."

The late Mr Hathaway had certainly had a point, Yvonne was thinking. But, oddly enough, she didn't feel upset at this stranger's idle chatter — quite the opposite, in fact.

It was soothing, even, to listen to this lonely, chatty stranger who'd known no cause to pity her — who, against her own circumstances, thought that Yvonne was lucky having Jilly.

As she took a bottle of milk from the fridge, she heard, through the open kitchen window, those small, impatient, clucking noises that Jilly always made prior to a bout of screaming.

Once more, her visitor apologised. "There, now, she's crying — and it's all my fault. I shouldn't have disturbed her."

Yvonne smiled briefly. "No, it isn't that. I expect she's getting bored — or hungry. I'll bring her inside."

Mrs Hathaway became so enthralled by Jilly crawling all over the carpet that she almost forgot about the milk she'd come to borrow . . .

94

"So silly of me, dear. Now, are you quite sure you can spare so much? You mustn't deprive your little girl, you know. She's the important one."

WHEN she'd seen Mrs Hathaway off at last, Yvonne walked thoughtfully back to the kitchen. Those last few words rang strangely in her ears.

She paused, alerted by the sudden silence. Where was Jilly? She moved around so quickly nowadays . . . Panic gripped her. You only had to leave a door ajar . . .

At the sound of gurgling and chuckling coming from Jenny's room, Yvonne went quickly to investigate. Jilly had pulled herself up against the bed, her chubby pink hands tugging at Jenny's wool.

"Oh, Jilly, darling — no!"

Suddenly, Yvonne stopped, aware that something was different. Jilly was standing — on her own!

Hearing Yvonne call out, Bob came rushing indoors, still with that anxious, guarded look. He glanced at Yvonne, surprised to find her smiling. She pointed, her finger pressed against her lips, and he followed the direction of her eyes.

Then he saw Jilly standing, unsupported, by the bed. Silently they looked on while their daughter, lurching precariously, took three triumphant steps across the room.

Bob caught her in his arms, hugging her closely to him. "You're Daddy's clever girl, aren't you, precious?"

With tears in her eyes, Yvonne sat down on Jenny's bed, smoothing the crumpled square of Jenny's knitting. Then she began to knit the last few rows.

Bob stood beside the window, still holding Jilly. A blackbird fluttered out of the lilac tree, and Jilly lunged forward, wriggling in his arms, for a better look, her round blue eyes alert with curiosity.

Looking lovingly at his baby daughter, Bob said softly, "She's pretty bright, isn't she, love — walking at ten months and all that?" Adding after the smallest of pauses, "At this rate, she'll soon be knitting blankets herself just like Jenny."

Yvonne answered carefully, her hands still occupied with Jenny's knitting, "Jilly won't ever be another Jenny, sweetheart. She's always going to be herself, just Jilly."

Yvonne could feel her mind releasing its bitterness . . . feel the warmth creeping back into her heart — into a heart full of love for their little girl . . . their lovely daughter, Jilly . . .

Slowly Yvonne cast off the last few stitches and looked steadily into Bob's eyes.

"You know Jilly's growing fast . . . and she'll be needing a lot more space now that she's walking . . .

"I think perhaps we'll give her Jenny's room. What do you think, Bob?"

And Bob smiled gently at his wife as he nodded in agreement. ∎

GIRL ON A PEDESTAL

by S. Wynne

**She was perfect, but
I didn't know what she saw in me
— and that was the cause of my
fall from grace!**

THIS was my first weekend without Samantha.
And a pretty dismal one it promised to be.

I sat moodily on the grass at the top of
Harmony Hill, in the park just outside the town, my
arms clasping my knees. It was a beautiful spring
day of white clouds, blue skies and sunshine.

All around me were couples; families with
children, lovers holding hands, older people with

walking-sticks who had made it to the top, fathers flying kites with their off-spring.

I seemed to be the only person on Harmony Hill on my own — the only person in the world, the way I felt.

At the party last night, Samantha and I had had a blazing row.

A lot of the other men there were real high-fliers, with incomes to match, expensive cars, five-bedroom houses, time-shares abroad and a smart line in chat as they swanned around in their designer suits.

One of them had asked Samantha to dance.

I'd watched jealously from the sidelines, knowing I couldn't possibly match that sort of competition.

I'm a design engineer, and I've spent most of my life up till now with my head buried in books, plans, specifications — all the sort of stuff no girl like Samantha could possibly be interested in.

I didn't buy expensive clothes or find social chit-chat easy, and my idea of a pleasant evening out was the pub or a good movie. But she knew that.

I had every intention of changing, now that I was established in a good job with the money coming in regularly, and had a girl to keep me up to scratch.

My future looked pretty rosy, as a matter of fact, with excellent prospects. Things looked brighter than I'd ever dared to believe.

But I still didn't have the nerve to tap this fellow on the shoulder and say something cool and masterful like, "She's with me."

Finally, when the record ended, they stood talking animatedly before wandering through to the room where a buffet was laid out.

WRETCHEDLY I thought back to the first time I'd encountered Sam. She's a secretary in my engineering firm, and I'd gone into her department for something and found her standing on a chair, pointing.

"It's a mouse!" she screamed. "I saw a mouse! Oh, please do something! They absolutely terrify me!"

I'd never previously considered Samantha Edwards as the timid Victorian Miss sort. She was tall and slender with gorgeous brown hair and was just about the most confident young lady I'd ever encountered.

I'd seen her around in the corridor and the canteen, even in the lift, but never actually spoken to her. To be honest, I thought she looked definitely out of my league.

Yet, here she was, scared of a mouse? With anyone else I'd have burst out laughing.

But the chance was too good to miss.

"Don't worry, I'll deal with it," I reassured her. "Which way did it go?"

I stamped my feet and rattled filing-cabinet drawers till I judged the creature would have taken the hint and made itself scarce. Then I put my arm round Samantha and lowered her carefully to the floor.

"I'll have a word with the caretaker," I promised the trembling girl.

My arm tightened round her. "Calm down, love," I whispered gently. "It was much more frightened than you were, believe me!"

Then I collected my wits sufficiently to suggest that as it was then lunch time, why didn't I take her to the nearest wine bar? This went so well I was emboldened to ask her to come out with me on Saturday night.

We'd been dating ever since, some six weeks or so. I was deliriously happy, deeply in love, and totally unable to believe my luck.

Why did this gorgeous girl pick me, Gordon Peters, 24, unmarried, clean, honest, sense of humour, but not the type to sweep a girl off her feet?

But apparently I was her type. At any rate, she admitted to not going out with anyone else, or at least nothing serious.

I longed to say, "Are you serious about me, Samantha?"

But somehow I couldn't get the words out. If she said no, I'd know I was wasting my time.

And what if she said yes . . . No, I just couldn't take the risk! This was the most important thing that had ever happened to me, and I didn't want to make a mess of it.

Six weeks wasn't long. I'd wait a while longer. When the right moment came, I'd know.

Our evenings together were so wonderful. I'd sit gazing at her over the restaurant table, then afterwards we'd walk for ages, hand-in-hand, just talking, then we'd take a taxi home.

When she snuggled up beside me in the cab, I wanted to tell her all that was in my heart — how much I loved her. But my tongue couldn't seem to find the words to express myself.

Then when I got home I'd think of all the things I'd wanted to say, and curse myself for not managing to get them out.

Next time, I'd think. Next time I really will — but next time somehow it wasn't any better.

THEN came this party. I didn't want to go, but Samantha had had this invitation from one of the salesmen at work, and was dying to show off a new dress she'd bought, so of course I said I'd tag along.

"But don't expect too much. I'm not a party man," I'd warned. "Back at college with a good crowd, well, that was different. Here, we'll neither of us know a soul."

"We'll soon make contact, you'll see," she'd assured me. "Don't be so defeatist, Gordon — you've a lot more going for you than you realise."

Well, that was nice, but I didn't really believe her.

So when this tremendously confident guy swept her up while I was away getting us drinks, all my self-doubts returned.

Finally I gave myself a shake, mentally, and followed them to the buffet. I hung around making it very clear I was her man.

In the end he took himself off, and Samantha fairly turned on me.

"Making a show of yourself!" she accused. "Why shouldn't I have a bit of fun? There wasn't any harm in it. You could have danced with somebody else yourself — the room's full of unattached girls."

"I happen to have come here with you," I retorted.

"Oh, you're impossible!" she stormed. "Just a doormat, that's all you are!"

"I could always leave."

"Why don't you then? I'll get a lift with someone — you needn't worry about me!" she hissed.

I could see we were collecting a fascinated crowd. I wanted to sink through the floor — or better still put her over my knee — but I just said in sarcastic tones, "You do that, then. I'm sure you'll have absolutely no problem," and left.

I hung around for a bit in case Samantha came and found me again — well, I wanted to make sure (without announcing it to the world) that she had enough money on her for a taxi.

But she disappeared into the swirling throng of dancers, so I finally gave up and sought out Colin, the man who'd invited us.

"I'm going — Sam wants to stay on," I told him. "Make sure she gets home safely, will you? Tell her I'll be at the flat."

Back at my flat, I sat up till dawn wondering if she'd phone.

She didn't.

SO here I was on this brilliant Saturday afternoon on Harmony Hill, wishing I was dead.

I'd told one of my flatmates where I was going in case Samantha phoned, but I didn't really expect her to.

I looked around me now at the kite-fliers on Harmony Hill.

All these confident fathers seemed to be doing pretty well, calling out breezy instructions to their young while paying out yards of line with authoritative jerks and twitches that sent the kites sailing away high above their heads, merrily flirting their tails.

I envied those lucky dads with all my heart.

Then I observed, quite close to me, a would-be kite-flier who actually didn't have a partner. A pretty little girl about five, she was, and she was

100

with an even prettier mum. The two were as alike as two peas in a pod — brown-skinned, bright-eyed, and happy.

A great wave of longing filled me. Why didn't I have a pair like that to go home to?

Then I became aware that all was not well with the two girls. However desperately the mother jerked and twitched, the wretched kite failed to take off.

With nothing else to do, I sat and watched.

The little girl noticed. I saw her tugging at her mother's hand, beseeching her.

Then she came racing across the grass towards me, gasping eagerly. "Can you fly my kite for me? I'm Poppy."

I got dubiously to my feet. I've never flown a kite in my life.

The mother came panting after her daughter, demanding with equally trusting candour, "You wouldn't, would you? We've tried and tried but I can't seem to get it to go. I'm Lisa."

"I'm Gordon," I said, adding doubtfully, "I don't know whether I can."

"Of course you can!" Poppy contradicted me impatiently, stamping her small, trainer-clad foot. "Daddy could if he was here, only he's working. You're a man, aren't you?"

Well, that did it. I was a man, and now if ever was the time to prove it.

"Give me the kite," I ordered in authoritative tones I barely recognised myself.

Praying to all the flying gods that be, I took the little craft and its gear into my hands and strode masterfully right up to the very top of the hill.

Somebody heard me. As I loosed off the reluctant dragon (for so it appeared it was), struggling to recall all I'd ever learnt about air currents, a lucky breeze magically lifted the kite and took it high in the air, gloriously floating, dancing away with great curvetting leaps and swoops.

"It's going!" an ecstatic Poppy screamed. "Look, it's going! The man's made it go!"

She raced along at my side, followed by her laughing mother.

Triumphantly I jerked, twitched and tugged just like all the other dads, with a feeling of achievement I hadn't experienced in years.

Finally my luck ran out and the kite plummeted to earth just before I ran out of breath.

The three of us flopped to the ground, laughing delightedly at each other.

WELL!" a well-known voice said right beside me. "Someone's enjoying himself, I see!"

I spun round. Yes, it was Samantha. Her eyes were sparkling with anger the way they had last night when she'd told me off.

Yesterday, I would have groaned, scrambled to my feet scarlet with embarrassment, blurting out helpless excuses. Today —

Today, I had successfully flown a kite for two delightful women, and I was feeling on top of the world.

"Yes, it's great!" I told Samantha happily. "Meet Lisa — Poppy. Girls — this is Samantha."

I saw Sam go quite white, obviously not believing her eyes and ears.

Lisa gave a big smile and said, "Hello, Samantha!"

Poppy squeaked. "He flew my kite for me, he's as clever as my daddy!"

Then Lisa looked at her watch.

"That reminds me — Daddy'll be home soon," she said. "We must be on our way, poppet."

Getting to their feet, they both said goodbyes and hope-we-meet-agains.

Samantha and I looked at one another.

"They're nice, aren't they?" I said defiantly.

"The three of you seemed to be getting along very nicely," Samantha returned, tight lipped.

I looked at her. There was something different about her today, though I couldn't put my finger exactly on what it was.

"Yes," I told her. "We were."

I looked straight at her. She wasn't my adored Samantha, any more, too precious to risk offending. I had a bone to pick with her, as my grandmother used to say.

"Got back from the party all right, did you?" I queried tartly.

She reddened, and curiously, she looked decidedly guilty.

"Colin put me in a taxi," she mumbled.

"Oh, he did? Good. No-one else offered to, then?"

There was silence.

"Why didn't you ring me?" I demanded. "Or come back to the flat?"

102

SUDDENLY she burst into tears.

I gazed at her helplessly, my new-found confidence ebbing away.

"I was scared," she gulped at last. "I thought you'd be angry.

"I wanted to make you angry," she sobbed. "Our relationship seemed to be getting nowhere. That's why I danced with that stupid man, then went to the buffet with him. But when you were angry, well, somehow it wasn't funny."

"Why did you want to make me angry?" I said at last.

This was all a bit above my head.

"You always treat me like eggshells, Gordon!" Samantha burst out, her eyes at last meeting mine.

"I want you to make the decisions!" she wailed. "I don't want to be put on a pedestal and worshipped. That time you chased the mouse — it was really great."

I didn't think I could be hearing properly. I took refuge in apology.

"Look, I don't know much about girls really," I confessed.

"There you go again!" Samantha said, angrily.

"Look, I'm not girls. I'm a girl!" she almost shouted. "Like, you're not men, you're a man, see? Why don't you find out about me?"

Her expression softened then. "A man," she whispered. "The one I picked, right?"

Birds sang, a rainbow arched across the sky, music played. I'll swear they did, and don't let anyone try to contradict me.

"I've been very stupid," I said humbly.

Then, looking at my most beautiful girl in the world, I added, "But all that's going to change, Samantha, as of this minute! How d'you feel about, er, flying a kite?"

I'd meant to say, "about marrying me," but this was a bit sudden and also public. But I would say it, and before the night was out.

"We haven't got a kite," Samantha said.

She grinned.

"So who cares?" I grinned back. "Race you to the top of the hill, and the loser gets kissed!"

This was one time I was quite sure I wouldn't be the loser. ■

New Boy In

by Leslie Cameron

IT was almost two weeks since we'd moved to Scotland from the South of England. Oh, why did you have to take that new job, Dad? I don't like it here.

Everyone at school talks with a funny accent and they don't play cricket.

I almost fell asleep in class today. Miss MacIntyre was droning on about some boring old Scottish battle. She tried to draw the scene on the blackboard — amazing swirls of blue and yellow.

I think the English were the yellows because everybody cheered when she drew big blue arrows right through all the yellow bits.

I was just drifting off into a smashing dream about captaining England in the World Cup when — "Colin," Miss MacIntyre's voice rang out, "what happened next?"

How was I supposed to know? I looked at the board, trying to make sense of all those blue and yellow streaks.

"Em — they scored in extra time," I blurted out.

The lads all burst out laughing. My face went red. I tried to play dumb hoping Miss MacIntyre would ask someone else.

No such luck.

She silenced the class then turned to me again. "Colin?" she asked again.

"I don't know," I replied quietly.

"Well, I'm afraid you never will," she said equally quietly, but firmly, "unless you stop day-dreaming and start listening."

I grimaced and looked down at my desk.

"OK, someone tell me," Miss MacIntyre addressed the class.

"The English army got a thrashing!" came the loud response.

Then they all started chanting "Scotland! Scotland!" as if they were at an international football match.

At that the bell rang. Miss MacIntyre sighed and told us to go for lunch. The problem with school is you have to go even when you don't want to.

It would have been great to bunk off on such a sunny afternoon, I thought on my way home, but that would probably have caused more trouble.

Lunch was a salad, because Mum was still busy getting organised.

I ate up quickly and left the house before she could "organise" me to help her.

As it was, I arrived back at school too early. It was boring standing around watching them all playing football and so I found a quiet corner to

Town

He felt so alone, an outcast in this strange place. That's why he had to rise to the challenge he'd been set . . .

wait until the bell went for afternoon lessons.

That silly girl with the long fair hair came up to me.

"Hello." She smiled timidly. "My name's Shona."

"Are you bragging or complaining?" I asked casually, but then, realising she didn't appreciate my sense of humour I added, "Hi, I'm Colin."

She stood beside me watching a couple of boys trying to fly a paper plane.

It wasn't even a proper paper aeroplane. It was made out of old newspaper. They were laughing their heads off every time it looped and swirled round in the breeze until it nose-dived into the grass beside me.

I picked it up to have a closer look at the design.

"HANDS off!" one of them shouted. That was Scott, who always seemed to have a bag of chips for his lunch.

"Suit yourself," I said, letting it drop.

That upset the other one, obviously Scott's minder.

"Watch it!" Bob yelled. "You've bent its wing!" he added, flashing me a look of disgust.

"So what?" I retorted. "It's only a piece of paper."

"You've ruined it!" Scott said accusingly.

"You can easily make another," I told him shortly.

"Bet *you* couldn't," Scott challenged.

" 'Course I could," I retaliated.

"Not like this one. Could he, Scott?"

"Don't talk daft," I scoffed. "Once I made a plane that flew ten times as far as that."

"Don't believe you!" Scott countered. "Paper planes can't fly two hundred yards."

"Mine could," I boasted, wishing immediately that I hadn't.

"Prove it," Bob pushed the damaged plane into my face. "Go on," he said. "Prove it!"

I pushed it away. "Needs proper paper," I hedged.

"English paper?" Bob challenged.

"Make it out of chippie paper if you want," Scott called after me generously, "but it's got to fly two hundred yards by Sunday!"

"Sunday? Where?" I called back.

"Doesn't matter," Scott answered. "Anywhere in the village."

Time to stand up to them. "Fine by me," I said, sounding more confident than I felt.

Sunday was three days away. They would have forgotten all about it long before then.

I turned away from them to find that Shona girl waiting for me again.

"Can you really make a plane fly two hundred yards?" she asked incredulously.

"Leave it out," I said, secretly pleased at her open admiration.

"You'll have to do it!" Shona ordered, suddenly becoming brisk.

"Who says?"

"Scott."

"I don't have to do what *he* says."

Shona sighed and gave me an odd kind of look that made me realise I couldn't back out now.

"I'll help you fly your plane in the park after tea if you like," she said, changing the subject.

"Eh? Oh, well . . . OK, then," I answered unenthusiastically.

Shona was on the doorstep at five o'clock sharp.

"Hold that," I told her, thrusting a plastic bag containing the paper planes into her hand. "I have to get Charlie — he's coming with us. He's my dog."

The park's in the old part of the village. There are swings with seats and tyres, a mini football pitch with solid wooden goals and an enormous slide.

"Are you going to fly it up and down the football pitch?" Shona inquired.

"No — I'll let it go from the top of the slide," I replied.

"Watch you don't fall!" she cried as I started up the steps.

I was glad I'd never had a sister. I couldn't live with that kind of nagging all day, every day . . .

There were three planes in the plastic bag. One was dart-shaped, one was an arrowhead and the other was a special design, a sort of rocket, made from a sheet of cartridge paper I'd found in Dad's desk.

Once I'd reached the top of the slide I let them go, one by one.

Each paper plane rose, hovered, soared again, then circled, before dipping and landing on the grass.

Old Charlie was running round in crazy circles while Shona marked the landing spot of each plane before calculating the distances reached with a steel measuring tape.

"Which went the farthest?" I yelled down to her.

"This one went twenty-five yards," she shouted back, holding up the arrowhead plane.

"Wait there — I'm coming down," I called, sliding down to join her.

Sitting on the end of the slide, we considered our next move.

"We need more wind . . ." I mused.

"So would a bit more wind make it fly two hundred yards then?" she asked innocently.

I nodded in reply and turned to look at her flushed face. She was quite pretty, I supposed, in a quiet way — not bad as girls went . . .

"I bet your London parks are much better than this," she said softly. "I expect you have ponds and ducks and things."

The way she said it made me smile. She seemed to think London was some pretty exciting place.

"Ever been to London?" I asked.

"No," Shona said, her eyes shining. "What's it like?"

I was looking around the open space, out across the rows of houses, tree-lined meadows, to the distant hilltops glowing dusty-golden in the setting sun.

"Well, it's a bit different from this," I replied. "Just a bit."

"I'd love to go there," she said wistfully as we packed up the planes and I whistled for Charlie to go home.

SUNDAY morning arrived and it wasn't raining. Scott and Bob were waiting for me at the end of the street, stuffing their faces with chocolate.

"Ready to show us your two hundred yards?" Scott gulped between bites.

"We want to see it fly — now!" Bob chimed in.

"Well, you'll have to wait," I said matter-of-factly. "I've got to get Shona first. She's my assistant."

Overhead, the sky was blue as we walked up to Shona's home in the new part of the village.

"Shona says that you can do it," Scott said, as if he didn't believe it.

"Tell us how then!" Bob panted, breathless from pushing Scott's bike up the hill.

I was grateful for Shona's undying faith. "Not right now," I said mysteriously. "Wait and see."

"Remember — it's now or never," Scott threatened, unwrapping another chocolate bar.

"No problem," I replied, trying to sound cool.

Shona's block of flats is 12 storeys high. It's also on a hill. Any wind about, they have it.

Shona lives on the 10th floor. She was standing on the balcony waving wildly to us. It made me dizzy just to look up at her.

"Now what?" Scott asked. Screwing up the paper from his chocolate bar, he tried to throw it at Shona. It went about five feet up in the air before the wind whipped it away.

"Wait here," I said, heading for the flats.

"Where're you off to now?" Scott wanted to know.

"Team talk," I said. "See you in a minute."

The lift went straight to the 10th floor. I rang the bell of number 10D.

A woman in a flowery dress opened the door. Shona was right behind her.

"Mum — this is Colin," she said shyly.

"Hello, Shona invited me up to see the view," I said, telling a tiny fib.

After taking me into the living-room, Shona slid the balcony door open. We stepped outside, looked down and waved to Scott and Bob.

"Ready!" I shouted down to them.

"Hey! That's cheating!" they yelled back.

"From anywhere in the village you said," I shouted, as I launched the arrowhead plane into space.

"Bet you can't find it!"

"Look how it flies!" we heard Bob yelling excitedly.

"Chase it! Catch it!" Scott, who was obviously impressed, screeched, running beside him.

From the balcony, Shona and I watched as the wind whipped up the paper plane and they chased it as it flew far away, across the car park towards the football pitch in the distance.

I turned to Shona. "It's gonna fly for ever!" I said, throwing back my head and laughing.

"Two hundred yards will do!" Shona replied as she turned to look at me, her eyes shining really brightly. I could tell she thought I was something pretty special. She was all right herself . . .

Maybe Scotland wasn't going to be so bad after all . . . ■

THE COLLIES

Out with the shepherd when the day is dawning,
    Running in dew in the early morning.
Chasing away the prowling fox
Whose bright eye covets the cherished flocks.
High in the hills where the eagles fly
And mistbound earth meets clouded sky
They hear on the wind an anguished cry.

At once they hurtle over the grass,
Into the mist that covers the pass.
A fox is watching a new born lamb
Lying helpless beside his terrified dam.
Into action at once, both dogs sparking,
With snap and snarl and an angry barking.

The fox flies off, baulked of his fun.
The ewe settles to suckle her new born son.
High on the hills where the eagles fly
And mistbound earth meets clouded sky
Two dogs, alert, a sound watch keep
The trusted guards who protect the sheep.

Joyce Stranger

Inspired by an illustration by Mark Viney

THE RELUCTANT HERO

She had the chance to follow her dream and he loved her too much to stand in her way.

by Sheila Ireland

IT was 2 a.m. Humphrey Bogart walked heroically across the tarmac and into the enveloping mist. The haunting strains of *As Time Goes By* were orchestrated once again to recapture the mood and the meaning of *Casablanca* and sadly the movie came to an end.

112

Jack Bradley uncurled his legs from the sofa, stood up, stretched and shook his head in admiration of the old movie.

He switched off the TV. The trouble with a movie like that, he thought, is you get so caught up in it. You don't get tired or want to go to bed. You want it to continue, to go on and on, and to take you with it.

The old movies had always been like that for him. They didn't seem old-fashioned at all, but more a thing of the future. To Jack, they seemed to say, *This is the way it can be.* He believed that, while the movie was running.

And for a time, the old movie loaned him its hope and its courage, and everything was made right in the end, the way it should be.

It was only afterwards that he began to feel vulnerable, as he did now.

He was a bit of a coward, really, he thought. Here he was, a 24-year-old bank teller in a one-bedroomed flat in a street without trees.

He did not look like Tom Cruise. He was not a dedicated sportsman and he had no talent that had made itself known.

He was not of the stuff of which heroes are made.

Jack knew that if he'd had any courage at all, he would have told Janet right at the start that he loved her, and asked her then if she was really sure about going to work in Australia. Couldn't she put it off for 10 years or so?

Australia was, after all, on the other side of the world, miles from anywhere. It was not a step to be taken lightly.

What was so attractive about kangaroos and koala bears and the back of beyond, anyway? Dear Old England had a lot more to offer, and it was cosy and friendly, wasn't it? You knew where you were here, didn't you?

He was glad he had decided to watch the movie in his pyjamas because now he could switch out the light and go straight to bed and sleep.

But getting to sleep wasn't so easy.

Jack couldn't block out the fact that Janet didn't even seem nervous about flying out to Australia.

As he lay in the darkness of his bedroom, he wondered if other people thought about their faults as much as he did about his.

He wondered if they put things off because they were nervous, thinking the delay would bring a new confidence. Or was it just him?

What would have happened if he had told Janet he loved her, right out, there and then, that very first night . . .?

It had been at a colleague's housewarming party that he'd met Janet. She'd come along with a girlfriend she had lost to an admirer at the door.

Janet stood alone for a long time, apparently not knowing what to do. Feeling sorry for her, he looked over and smiled and said hello.

He had walked her home that night. He thought she was very lovely and couldn't get over his good fortune. He'd never had much of a way with girls, before, but with Janet it was different.

113

She told him she was a nurse at the General and, no, it wasn't as romantic as they made it out to be, but something she had always wanted to do.

When she finished her training she was going to Australia, she said happily, to the sunshine of Sydney where her big brother was a computer analyst and married with two little girls she had never even seen.

And like an idiot and the bank clerk he was, he said, "Great. But won't that be expensive? The flight, I mean."

Janet smiled easily. "Yes. But I'm paying for my ticket now, a little every week, you know. They let you do that at World Travel, the agency on Barber Street . . ."

Jack sighed and told himself to go to sleep. He had a momentary vision of Humphrey Bogart saying goodbye in *Casablanca*. The airport and the mist. It was funny how it helped block out the deceitful part of his mind and let the truth loose.

He forced himself to face the cold facts. He loved Janet. He had always loved Janet and he had to think of what was best for her.

If her heart was set on Australia, then that was that. There was nothing he could do about it.

AT that point, the phone rang. Jack got up and switched on the light and went back into the lounge.

"Hello, Jack." It was Janet. Her voice sounded warm and tired and husky. "Jack, did you watch it?"

Jack smiled. He was glad to hear her voice.

He said, "The movie? Yes. Loved it. You know me and the old movies, Janet. Did you enjoy it?"

"Yes. Lovely. Sad but lovely." Janet paused and put distance between them for a moment. Then she gave a long yawn and said, "Oh, I'm sorry, Jack. I should be in bed. Jack, remember you're meeting me in town tomorrow. At two, all right?"

"Don't worry, I'll be there. Janet, you're not having second thoughts, last-minute regrets, maybe changing your mind, uh?"

"No, Jack."

Jack took a breath. "OK. See you at two."

Back in bed, sleep came no more easily. He couldn't get Janet and Australia out of his mind. Just a few days to go now . . .

It was a long flight. He hoped she wouldn't get air sick.

Jack tossed and turned and tried to get comfortable but it was no use.

What was the big deal about going to Australia, anyway?

All right, it had the weather. He couldn't deny that. Sunshine and surfing, he had to admit, were pleasures one had to forego if one lived in England. But . . .

England. The green fields and the cosy, country pubs. London and the Changing of the Guard. The Monarchy. The Queen, God Bless 'er.

He almost hummed a few bars of *Land Of Hope And Glory* to bolster up his conviction, his spirit, his pride and patriotism.

114

Yet when he thought of Janet it all seemed different.

"Go to sleep," he muttered irritably. He forced himself to think of the old movie, and ran it through again in his mind.

Bogart was sitting with a drink at the bar, thinking of the woman he loved, the woman he would bravely give up, listening to the man playing their song on the piano . . .

THE next day, Jack walked heroically down the street on the way to meet Janet.

He was thinking heroic thoughts, like how he would never stand in the path of Janet's happiness. He would never take away her dream of a whole new life, he loved her too much.

It made him feel like Bogart.

Only he was smiling, and when he saw Janet he waved and broke into a trot.

He was no hero.

It had taken him a whole six months to pluck up the courage to tell Janet he loved her. Another four months to finish paying off his instalments at the World Travel Agency . . .

Janet held out her hand as he approached and he took it and squeezed it tightly.

She returned the squeeze, but her eyes, when she looked up at him, held an expression Jack had never seen in them before.

Apprehension.

He smiled gently as he pulled her towards him and felt her relax slightly as she whispered, "Oh, Jack, are we really doing the right thing?"

Were they? He'd been tortured by doubts all night. It wasn't too late to draw back — and now, for the first time, he felt he might be able to draw Janet back with him.

They could stay in England, get married immediately, buy a cosy, semi-detached villa somewhere in the suburbs, ideal for commuting . . .

That had been his dream. But he knew it had never been Janet's . . .

Again he smiled down at Janet, a confident smile now. "Yes, of course we're doing the right thing."

It was truly heroic. And his reward came in her answering smile, a smile of such radiance and love that Jack felt just a little over ten-feet tall.

Lowering his left eye in what he fondly imagined to be a Bogart-like wink, he murmured, "Here's looking at you, kid," before leading her into the travel agency.

Now, as he held their airline tickets in his hand, Jack felt like a man of destiny. Courage coursed through his veins. For the first time in his life, he'd been Bogart.

But as he and Janet walked outside and made their way down the street, arm-in-arm and happy as two love-birds, oddly enough he wasn't whistling *As Time Goes By.*

It was another little ditty called *Waltzing Matilda.* ■

A Very Important

by Pauline Gaffney

For all his tender years, he'd learned that if he gave his heart, it was bound to be broken.

ROBBIE gazed out through the living-room window, his 10-year-old face a study in calculated indifference, staring unseeing at the rows of brightly-coloured dahlias at the bottom of the garden.

Instead he conjured up a picture of the blocks of flats where he'd lived for the first few years of his life. Dingy it may have been, even ugly, but it was the only real home Robbie had known.

Setting his face more firmly into its deadpan expression, he drew back from the window to look around the comfortable room.

She would be back any minute now, bringing cakes and drinks from the kitchen. Well, he would eat them all right.

Funnily enough, the "Home" where he lived didn't go in much for home-baking.

Yes, he would certainly eat them, but she wouldn't get round him as easily as that. He allowed himself a tiny smirk of satisfaction at his own resourcefulness.

If there was one thing he had learned, it was how to be tough . . . not to let anybody near enough to hurt him.

It worked, too. It was ages since he'd cried — he could hardly remember the last time. The matron at the Home didn't like the fact that he bottled up his emotions — Robbie knew that. She'd talked to him about it once or twice.

"Robbie, dear," she would say in her low, quiet voice, "don't be afraid to show your feelings . . . being lonely or afraid isn't a weakness, you know."

Him — scared? What a nerve! And how did she know he felt lonely or frightened? Nobody knew, he made sure of that . . .

His thoughts returned to the cosy living-room. He could hear *her* clattering about in the kitchen. She sounded happy . . . she was humming a tune — no doubt thinking how nice it was to have a boy about the house — until she got tired of him, that was.

Secretly, Robbie thought she didn't look too bad . . . or her husband either, for that matter. They were about 30, with nice, friendly faces . . .

116

Lesson

She was pretty with curly hair and a big smile. He was tall and slim and wore glasses.

But Robbie didn't allow such considerations to side-track him. Once he let his guard down and trusted them, they would ditch him — just like Mum had ditched him years ago . . .

It had been just after Dad died that Mum had become ill. They'd called it a "breakdown" or something.

Anyway, she'd had to go away for a long time, more than a year. And, as there was nobody else to look after him, Robbie had gone to the Home.

117

After the first time, he hadn't even been allowed to visit Mum in hospital. Apparently she'd been really upset when she'd seen him. He'd overheard the doctors saying he reminded her of her late husband, and so it might be as well if she didn't see him . . . for a while.

When Mum had started to get better, she'd come to fetch him. But somehow he hadn't known her any more. She'd been like a pale, silent stranger, and all the closeness there had been between them seemed to have vanished.

But she had taken him home, to a flat she'd acquired — not the one where they'd lived when Dad was alive, but a tiny modern one in a different part of town. And she had tried to look after him . . . but, in reality, she could hardly look after herself.

Many a day she'd forget to cook any tea for them, and Robbie had rarely had a clean shirt or jumper for school.

Or else she would suddenly go off and spend all her housekeeping money on a new dress or a bright rug for the flat.

Then there would be nothing in the cupboard to eat until the next lot of money, with the result that she was forced to scrounge off neighbours.

But worse than this were the days when she'd sit quiet and still, gazing into the fire all day. She hadn't bothered to take Robbie to school on those occasions, in fact, she hardly seemed aware that he was there at all.

IT was because of these absences from school that the situation had come to light. A teacher had called round and alerted the school's social worker. Then it was back to the Home for Robbie, and back to the hospital for his mum.

That was the first time he'd heard the words "long-term fostering". He hadn't known what they meant, and he hadn't cared.

It was a relief to be back in the security of the Home, and he still hoped that his mother would get back to her old self sometime and be able to love him and make a home for him again.

But, though she'd visited him from time to time, she'd been more distant than ever. And on one visit she'd even gone into a long, rambling explanation of how she couldn't take on any sort of responsibility, any more, and needed looking after herself.

And wasn't he glad, she asked him, that she had found someone to care for her? She would never forget him, she assured him, but it was better this way . . .

Robbie had had no idea what his mother was talking about, and had to rely on the matron to explain it all after she'd gone.

As gently as she could, Matron had told him that his mother was about to remarry; the man was an Australian, she'd confided, putting her arm round Robbie' shoulders as she told him they would be moving there to live . . . without Robbie.

THAT night he'd cried himself to sleep; but he had learned a valuable lesson, and he determined never to cry again; never to rely on anybody else for love or affection in case they let him down the way his mother had done.

He'd repeated the lesson over to himself several times to fix it in his head.

Various people had shown an interest in Robbie over the years. But his total refusal to co-operate in any way soon put them off — until this woman with the fluffy hair had come along with her husband . . .

In fact, Robbie had been quite surprised that they had noticed him at all. After all, he had been in the same room as a beautiful, fair-haired baby girl, and a two-year-old boy with huge, dark eyes and a happy smile.

However, they'd walked right past these two and come over to where Robbie had sat hunched in front of the TV set. Quickly he'd run his hands through his untidy, sandy hair and licked his lips nervously. His eyes darted suspiciously from one to the other as the man and woman had begun speaking.

They were looking for someone to share their home, they'd told him gently. They especially wanted someone who'd had a hard time, who needed love and understanding.

They didn't want him to commit himself right away, though . . . and so perhaps he'd like to come to stay for the odd weekend to give them all the chance to get to know each other . . . to see if they'd get along together all right . . .

Robbie had listened in silence, unable to think of anything to say in response. And, because he hadn't been able to find a reason for refusing quickly enough, he'd found himself agreeing to spend the odd weekend with the Wests.

The weekends were OK . . . nice bedroom all to himself . . . comfortable bed where he could read with the light on as long as he liked . . . good meals, visits to the seaside — and, to Robbie's relief, not too much boring talking and endless questions.

That was the one thing Robbie couldn't stand, people going on and on at him about how they wanted to make him happy, and what a good home they were going to give him, just as if he hadn't any say in the matter at all.

They seemed to think that just because they'd decided to *make* him happy, he'd automatically *become* happy, just like that. It irritated him.

But this Mrs West — or Belle as she'd asked him to call her — wasn't like that. Neither was Mr West. They'd chatted in a nice, easy way about all sorts of things — television programmes, football teams, books they'd read. But they hadn't pried into his past or gone all emotional on him.

THAT'S why he'd found himself sitting in their living-room again. He'd agreed to go back for yet another visit.

119

While Belle was preparing an afternoon snack, he'd reminded himself to keep her at arm's length, so that he could go on enjoying the visits until the Wests got fed up with him. And when they did, he wouldn't get hurt.

"It's ready!" Belle called, interrupting his train of thought as she pushed open the door with one foot and carried in a tray.

"I thought you might be hungry after the journey, Robbie, so I made you a couple of hot-dogs."

Robbie's eyes lit up as he took a plate with a hot-dog off the tray, but his voice was the usual monotone when he answered.

"Thanks," he mumbled, mindful of Matron's instructions.

"Mike will be back soon," Belle continued conversationally, picking up her mug of tea. "Then we can plan what to do this weekend." She paused in case Robbie wanted to suggest anything, but as he continued eating in silence she said:

"What about the cinema this evening? There's a good adventure film on in town."

"OK," Robbie agreed, deliberately keeping any enthusiasm out of his voice. He would have said OK whatever had been suggested.

Once you started discussing things, getting excited and all that, it was no good. You were like part of a family then, and you felt worse than ever when they decided to ditch you.

He'd seen it happen to children at the home once or twice.

Belle was talking again . . .

"How do you fancy a trip to a safari park tomorrow, Rob?" She called him Rob every now and again and he liked it. It made him feel more grown-up somehow.

"Yeah . . . all right," he said carelessly. He felt suddenly apprehensive . . . He'd never been to a safari park before. He'd heard there were lions wandering about. Well, there was no way he was getting out of the car . . .

The weekend passed as weekends with the Wests usually did . . . calmly, undemandingly, with plenty of food and the minimum of fuss. Even the lions hadn't been as frightening as he'd expected.

When Belle dropped him off at the Home on Sunday evening she leaned across to open the car door and let him out.

For a split second Robbie thought she was going to hug him or kiss him goodbye — something she'd never yet done. And when she didn't, an unreasonable feeling of emptiness washed over him.

"See you next weekend, Rob," she called brightly as he scrambled out, adding quickly, " — if you feel like it, of course."

He'd grunted a reply before disappearing up the gravel drive and through the doorway of the Home.

HOWEVER, the following week there was a phone call on the Friday evening to say the Wests couldn't come for him that weekend. In spite of his disappointment, Robbie was almost pleased in a perverse way. It had shown he'd been right about them ditching him in the end.

Well . . . tough! At least he hadn't started to love them or anything. If he had, he told himself, he would be feeling really rotten by now — really miserable and let down.

He brushed his sleeve across his eyes and sniffed. He hadn't let them hurt him, but he still felt rotten, somehow.

It was two more weeks before he saw anything of the Wests, though they had sent several messages to assure him they hadn't forgotten him.

It seemed that Belle had been ill, and they were truly sorry to have disappointed him by not having him to visit.

"Huh . . ." Robbie had said when Matron passed on the information. And that was all she could get out of him.

However, on the third weekend, there was another message to say they were coming for him if he was agreeable.

He looked so sullen that Matron felt obliged to say, "You do want to go, Robbie, don't you?" Staring past her head at the trees outside the window, he shrugged his shoulders.

"I don't mind . . . yeah, all right then," he said grudgingly.

He was quite shocked when the car pulled up at the door and Belle got out. She had dark smudges under her eyes and her skin was a papery-white.

For the first time it occurred to him that they had been telling the truth . . . Belle really had been ill. His spirits lifted at the realisation that they hadn't lied.

But despite this encouraging sign, he remained cautious. It was too soon to drop his guard yet. Settling himself in the car, he sat silently until they reached the house.

"Rob," Belle said tentatively, while Mike was making coffee, "would you mind if we just spent a quiet weekend in? I'm not quite up to gadding about yet . . ." she smiled ruefully, and he allowed himself a glimmer of a smile in return.

"It's OK with me," he mumbled, not meeting her eyes.

It was a very pleasant weekend, to his surprise — all the more so because they *didn't* do anything. Mike hired a science-fiction video and while they watched it, Belle sat on the sofa resting and doing a jigsaw.

Robbie enjoyed helping her to find the pieces — in fact, he was rather good at spotting which went where. And, one or twice, while they were fitting the pieces in position, he actually found himself relaxing and forgetting to keep up his guard.

THE next time he went for his weekend visit, the Wests had some shattering news for him.

"We're going to have a baby," Belle said, her wide smile lighting up her face. "Isn't that great news, Rob? That's why I was a bit under the weather the other week."

"Great," Robbie said flatly, his heart plummeting to his boots. So that

121

was that. I would be goodbye to the Wests now that they were having a kid of their own.

He was angry with himself . . . They had got through his defences in spite of all his efforts to keep them out. There was an ominous pricking of tears behind his eyes. Life was the pits sometimes, he mused bleakly.

"Rob," Belle said seriously, later in the evening, as they put the last few pieces in the jigsaw, "there's something we have to discuss with you, now that there's a baby on the way."

Here it comes, Robbie thought, bracing himself for the brush-off. Well, he would beat them to it.

"It's all right," he shouted, jumping to his feet and upsetting the completed puzzle. "I don't care if you don't want me here . . . I never wanted to come in the first place."

Mike stared at him with a horrified look on his gentle, caring face. And Belle looked as though someone had hit her. Robbie didn't like to see them looking like that.

"I'll go and get my things," he muttered in a quieter voice, gulping down a rising sob.

"Oh no you won't!" Mike said, blocking Rob's exit. "What's the big idea, Rob? I thought we were all getting on so well."

"You don't need me now you're having your own kid," he replied, heading for the door.

"Rob," Belle said softly, "come here — please, love." He half turned and saw that her eyes were bright with tears. Slowly he walked across to the sofa.

"What Mike and I wanted was a family . . . and as soon as you came to stay with us, that was what we felt we had — a real family." She paused for breath, while Robbie brought his gaze up to meet hers.

"Right from the start we wanted you to stay with us permanently . . . and now that the baby is on the way we want that more than ever. Mike and I . . . we love you, Rob," she said hesitantly, her voice trembling.

Robbie stared at her closely, his face pink with excitement and embarrassment. It was a long time since anybody had told him they loved him. Was she having him on? He looked round at Mike. He was smiling reassuringly.

"We'd like you to make this your home, son, but only if it's what you want," he said quietly.

Robbie turned back to Belle, the excitement pushing through all the barriers he'd built up.

"Do you mean it?" he asked, hardly daring to breathe.

"We mean it," she answered solemnly, looking steadily into his eyes. Robbie was right beside her now, as she held out her arms to hug him.

For a long moment he hesitated. Once he went into those welcoming arms, there could be no turning back . . . he would have shown them he cared, that he needed their love . . .

"Yeah . . . OK . . . I'll stay," he said gruffly, walking into Belle's outstretched arms. ■

122

MIDSUMMER MADNESS

by Marian Hipwell

Strange, but it was the ridiculous feud between their families that actually brought them together.

A STATE of discord had existed between the Grey family at No. 12 Keeler Close and the Dawson family at No. 19 ever since Thomas Dawson, an enthusiastic gardener, with an impressive marrow in the vegetable section, had taken first prize at the local fête; and that in the face of strong competition from the equally enthusiastic Jack Grey and his particularly succulent tomatoes.

It was a pity about the rift because the families really had so much in common. The wives both worked part time at the local market; Celia Grey on the confectionery stall while Jeannie Dawson helped out at the bacon stall.

The Greys' seven-year-old son, John, and the Dawsons' daughter, Trudy, were in the same class at primary school, even though they had contrived to sit at opposite ends of the classroom.

The Dawsons' elder son, Rod, worked in a local bank, and the Greys' daughter, Sally was doing her "A"-levels.

Recently Rod had become more and more aware of how attractive that quiet Sally Grey from down the road was becoming. She, too, had begun to take notice of the tall young man who often jumped off the No. 11 bus in front of her on a Saturday morning and turned in at the gate of No. 19.

Brief glances had been exchanged, yet both were mindful of the feud between their respective families, and so kept their distance.

The families even had similar pastimes and hobbies. Most weekends, in summer, the Grey family piled into their car and headed for the coast, where they had a caravan; the Dawsons, too, would often decide to get away from it all and drive off to a country camp-site where they'd pitch their tent.

THINGS might have gone on in much the same fashion, had it not been for the local Annual Summer Fête; the same fête where, in the later summer of a previous year, the Dawson marrow had triumphed over the Grey tomatoes.

Since then, both families had pointedly avoided the occasion, yet by some strange quirk of fate, both Jack Grey and Thomas Dawson had decided, unbeknown to the other, that this was the year that they would make their come-back.

Jack had abandoned vegetables in favour of flowers; his sweet-smelling roses were said to have the largest heads in the district.

Wisely, Thomas had also had a change of heart. His colourful petunias were a superb example of horticultural expertise.

Encouraged by her daughter, Sally, Celia Grey had decided, for the first time, to enter the cake competition — friends and family alike could vouch that her strawberry gâteau was second to none.

Jeannie Dawson, too, was going in for the competition with her light, fluffy angel cake — another confirmed family favourite.

To further complicate matters, there was to be an additional feature this year; a children's pet show, and young John Grey was particularly keen to enter his puppy, Sylvester, a lively little rascal of uncertain ancestry, who had, so far, defied all attempts at training.

On hearing the news of the pet show, little Trudy Dawson had lost no time in entering Sheba, her delightful kitten, who lacked Sylvester's liveliness, but had the edge on him in looks.

The stage was set, it seemed, for a confrontation which would echo round Keeler Close for a long time to come . . .

At precisely ten o'clock, on the morning of the fête, Thomas Dawson, accompanied by his wife bearing her angel cake aloft, and young daughter, Trudy, clutching her bewildered cat to her chest, left their house and headed for the fête.

Reluctantly, Rod Dawson walked behind them, resigned now to the idea of spending his precious Saturday morning at what he considered would be a decidedly boring affair.

From his lofty 20 years, he regarded the feudal situation, which existed between his own parents and the Grey family, as rather childish, yet loyalty made him support his own.

He knew something, too, which he would rather not have known, and it weighed heavily on his conscience this morning.

Some moments later, the Grey family followed suit, Jack Grey bearing his magnificent roses in front of him casting an anxious eye at the breeze which had sprung up, while Celia Grey proudly clutched her carefully-boxed cake to her.

Sylvester, warned to be on his best behaviour for the duration of the fête, trotted along merrily at young John's side.

Sally Grey followed unenthusiastically. She was the unwilling holder of a secret and, because of it, she would rather have given the whole affair a miss. Yet, loyalty to her family sent her hurrying after them at the last moment.

By the time they arrived, many of the stalls had already been set up and were groaning under the weight of colourful garden produce and riotous displays of flowers.

THE cake stall was a sight to behold. Creative chocolate concoctions looked down on slabs of pink and white coconut ice, while Swiss rolls jostled for space alongside neat rows of identical fairy cakes and perfectly-formed raspberry buns.

Mrs Dawson's angel cake was placed temptingly near the front of the stall, but, from the moment Celia Grey placed her light, creamy, strawberry gâteau among the contenders, the result of the competition was a foregone conclusion.

The cake was given pride of place on a silver cake stand, from where it looked down in a superior fashion on the lesser offerings at the fête.

Mrs Grey beamed shyly, then, as she caught her daughter, Sally's, eye, she looked quickly away.

For a potential prize-winner's daughter, Sally looked unusually disturbed as she turned away from the cake stall.

"Congratulations! Well, to your mother, at any rate. She's bound to win with that amazing cake!"

She turned at the voice beside her. Rod Dawson was standing there, smiling hesitantly at her.

At first she frowned, then found herself returning his infectious smile.

"Thanks," she murmured. She couldn't help noticing his warm brown eyes. He lingered, eyeing her shyly.

"Pretty boring, this kind of occasion," he remarked. "I usually spend Saturday morning in the sports centre, myself."

"Do you? I go there myself quite a lot. Haven't seen you there, though. What game do you play?"

"Squash," he told her.

"Oh." She smiled self-consciously. "Swimming's my sport."

Without either of them realising it, they had fallen into step, and were walking slowly in the direction of the refreshment tent.

"Don't suppose you fancy an ice-cream or a drink, or something?" he asked tentatively. Sally hesitated.

"I wouldn't mind a cold drink," she admitted. "It's getting hot."

He grinned at her, looking relieved.

"Right. Come on, then! I'm thirsty, too."

Conflicting emotions crossed Sally's mind as they walked together towards the tent.

"Actually, my parents won't be too pleased to see me talking to you, you know," she told him confidentially, looking over her shoulder to see if they were watching.

"Mine won't be exactly overjoyed either," he replied cheerfully. "But it's all a bit silly, isn't it?" he added, as they reached the entrance to the tent.

She returned his smile and nodded in agreement.

"I think it's crazy!"

126

As they entered the refreshment tent, they passed a group of people who had to be the judges for the various competitions.

In the marquee where the pet show was being held, people were gathered — waiting, trying desperately, and mostly unsuccessfully, to control pets weary of being on their best behaviour for so long.

Young Trudy Dawson had arrived late with her kitten in the tent and was searching anxiously for a place.

From across the room, young John Grey glowered at her, as he held on to the, by now, exceedingly fractious Sylvester.

Despite her frantic searching, the only place available to Trudy for her pet was next to that of her adversary — John Grey.

As soon as she deposited Sheba on the exhibition stand next to Sylvester, trouble broke out between them.

Sheba spat at Sylvester. Sylvester barked at her, and the rest of the pets, already restive, joined in with gusto.

Horrified, Trudy made a grab for Sheba just as young John Grey lunged towards his puppy. Alas, both were too late.

Sheba's tail shot up in the air as Sylvester took a mighty leap towards her, overturning the exhibition stand and causing widespread commotion in the tent as gerbils gibbered and budgies fluttered in alarm.

Of Sheba and Sylvester there was now no sign.

In hot pursuit, both Trudy and John glimpsed Sylvester speeding towards the marquee entrance, and it was a fair bet that not far in front of him was the pride of the Dawson household.

SYLVESTER caught up with his quarry by the cake stall. In an effort to evade him, Sheba jumped on to the table, scattering fruit flans and chocolate rum truffles everywhere.

High on its silver cake-stand, Celia Grey's sumptuous strawberry gâteau, leading contender for the culinary rosette, tottered under the impact of scrambling paws.

Amid cries of horror, people leapt forward to save the cake but alas — they were too late. The splendid cake, knocked from its elegant perch, crashed to the ground in a shower of flying crumbs and dollops of cream.

Neither pet lingered to witness the result of their mad dash. Sylvester had eyes for only his quarry, and Sheba's one thought was to escape from her predator.

Across the field they streaked, paying no heed to the obstacles in their path nor the frenzied attempts of onlookers to catch them.

In the horticultural section, people were waiting expectantly for the judging to begin, Thomas Dawson carefully avoiding Jack Grey's accusing stare. The affair of the marrow died hard, it seemed . . .

Suddenly, into the middle of the rostrum darted a small grey cat, followed by an enraged, and only slightly larger, black puppy. Narrowly missing Jack Grey's prize roses, they plunged headlong into Thomas Dawson's treasured petunias.

A cry of anguish broke from Thomas as he saw the havoc the two creatures had wreaked among his blooms. To add insult to injury, Sylvester, evidently captivated by the flowers, paused in his pursuit of the cat for just long enough to make a quick meal of them.

In a trice, the petunias were gone and Thomas Dawson was out of the competition.

Bedlam broke out, yet in the melée which followed, Jack Grey, alone, had the foresight to pick up his blooms and hold them aloft out of harm's way. Then the dog and cat were off again, leaving the exhibitors to survey the chaos they'd left in their wake.

"Your dog —" Thomas Dawson's voice quivered with emotion and suppressed rage when he finally managed to speak "— has eaten my petunias!"

"And your cat —" Celia Grey screamed, her face white with fury and her mouth trembling "— has totally destroyed my strawberry gâteau!"

Back in the refreshment tent, unaware of the drama being enacted by their respective families, Rod Dawson and Sally Grey were embarking on their third drink and rapidly feeling sufficiently at ease with one another to exchange confidences.

"Why do our parents have to behave so ridiculously?" Sally mourned.

"I don't know," Rod answered. "I've no patience with them — they're so childish." He hesitated, then leaned towards Sally, lowering his voice.

"Dad shouldn't have won that year really, you know."

"Oh?" Sally eyed him doubtfully.

"No, he shouldn't." He shook his head. "It wasn't really his marrow." Relieved that the weight of guilt was lifted, he met her enquiring gaze.

"I'm only telling you because — well, we aren't like them, are we?"

"Definitely not." She spoke determinedly. "Whose marrow was it, then?" she asked after a moment.

"My Uncle Ian's. Not that my dad cheated deliberately, you understand!" he added hastily. "But his own marrows weren't coming on at all well and Uncle Ian felt sorry for him.

"He substituted one of his own the night before the fête and Dad didn't realise until it was all over." Sally stared at him.

"You mean he didn't notice the difference in the size of the marrow overnight?" she asked incredulously.

"Uncle Ian told him he'd put some special, quick-acting fertiliser on

128

the marrows," Tom told her gravely. "I know it sounds ridiculous but I expect Dad wanted to believe it.

"He intended to hand the rosette back when he discovered the truth, but he was so embarrassed. And he'd been bragging so much about it to all and sundry." His voice held youthful scorn.

"Well! That was a disgraceful, rotten thing to do," Sally said indignantly. "That was cheating. And your uncle was just as bad playing a trick like that!"

"I know, Sally." He sighed heavily. "I agree entirely." She took a long sip of her drink.

THEY sat in companionable silence for a while then suddenly Sally spoke.

"It isn't really my mother's strawberry gâteau, you know," she confided.

"Oh?" It was Tom's turn to be surprised as, shamefacedly, Sally explained.

"I wish I didn't know about it," she said miserably, "but I came home early last night, to find Mrs Robinson from the confectioner's stall — where Mum works — helping her decorate the cake.

"Even though it was made on our premises, technically, it's Mrs Robinson's cake." She gave a helpless gesture.

"Mum's effort was a flop and she panicked and rang Mrs Robinson for advice. But what happens? Round comes Mrs Robinson who then makes the whole thing for her!

"Mum shouldn't have let her but she was tired and fed up after her disaster." Rod was speechless for a moment.

"She could have withdrawn," he protested at last.

"Like your dad?" Sally eyed him spiritedly. "Anyway, Dad's been singing her praises to everybody, telling them what a marvellous baker she is. Well, she is, normally. She didn't want to lose face with him either, I suppose.

"So I agreed to say nothing. And she didn't really expect her cake to win, you know."

"Well, she doesn't seem to have much competition from what I saw," Rod muttered.

"Yes, it was the best cake there by a mile." Sally spoke glumly. "I know you won't tell anyone what I've told you." It was his turn to look troubled.

"Of course I won't say anything!" he insisted. "Just as I know you'll keep quiet about Uncle Ian's marrow. And anyway, I'm glad we're above such things," he said conspiratorially.

The good atmosphere restored between them, they smiled happily at each other. Rod cleared his throat.

"I heard someone saying there's a disco at the sports centre tonight."

"That's right," Sally said brightly. "I'm going — are you?"

"I think I might go . . . could we go together?" he asked tentatively.

Sally nodded happily as he looked hopefully into her eyes.

"Hey, I wonder how the competitions are going?" Rod said, suddenly remembering why they were there. "Fancy finding out?"

"All right, but I've a feeling that whoever wins, there's bound to be trouble."

With that, they walked back towards the main part of the fête.

"Oh, no!" Rod nudged Sally, as they approached.

HIS father and hers were standing, some feet apart, outside the main marquee.

Jack Grey was holding a large yellow rosette, and Thomas Dawson was eyeing it angrily.

Celia Grey stood by her husband, a supportive hand on his arm, and at Thomas's side was his devoted wife, Jeannie.

Trudy Dawson, catching sight of her older brother, hurried over to him. Rod and Sally listened, with growing horror, as the whole sorry tale unfolded.

"Oh, great!" Sally sighed, when it was finished. "Where are the two animals now?"

"Shut up in disgrace in the cars," Trudy informed her.

Rod eyed the two sets of parents uneasily as they made their way across to them. His father, somewhat pink in the face by now, was muttering darkly, casting grim looks at Sally's dad.

"That rosette was gained on false pretences," they could hear him grumbling, while Celia Grey was looking daggers at the rosette-bedecked angel cake which Jeannie Dawson was holding aloft.

"That cake won by default!" Celia snapped.

"My cake won because it was the best one there!" Jeannie retorted.

"Justice has been seen to be done!" Rod murmured, looking on.

"Eh? What's that, lad?" His father glanced in his direction, and Rod

130

cast an agonised look at Sally. Under her encouraging glance, he turned back to his father.

"I was just saying Uncle Ian would have approved of Mr Grey's giant blooms." He eyed his father steadily. He was aware then of Sally's fingers slipping into his own.

"And I bet Mrs Robinson, at the market, would rate your mum's cake delicious," she added innocently.

There was a lengthy silence, during which time both Thomas Dawson and Celia Grey underwent sudden changes of colour and of heart.

"Oh, well, it's only a competition," Thomas said at last, looking straight at Jack Grey. "And your roses were top class," he added generously.

"And I must admit I'm rather partial to angel cake," Celia Grey chipped in, avoiding her daughter's eye.

"Fancy that," Sally said demurely.

"Why not pop across later and try a slice?" Jeannie Dawson asked unexpectedly.

"Well, that's very kind of you!" Celia Grey responded, surprised and delighted at the invitation. "What do you think, Jack?"

"I think it's bound to taste better than those petunias did," he chuckled.

THE two couples began to move towards the gate, smiling self-consciously at each other.

"Who won the pet show in the end, Trudy?" Sally asked, remembering. Trudy scowled.

"Freddie Taylor's budgie," she said disgustedly. "And it can't even talk!"

As they began to move towards their respective cars, young John Grey peered round his mother's skirts at Trudy Dawson.

"Well, I don't care what anybody says, I still don't like you!" he declared frostily, glaring at Trudy.

"That's enough of that!" his father intervened.

"Children!" His mother shook her head, sighing.

"Grown-ups!" John sighed.

They all looked at each other, then there was a burst of laughter all round. And that was how the feud of Keeler Close was finally settled once and for all.

And when, in the fullness of time, Celia Grey walked down the aisle arm in arm with Thomas Dawson, followed by Jeannie Dawson and Jack Grey, their eyes resting proudly on their radiant offspring, the new Mr and Mr Rod Dawson, no-one would have believed that the two families had ever been anything else but the very best of friends . . . even if the two youngest members of the respective families were glowering at each other over the pews . . . ■

STRANGERS ON

by Cheryl Morgan

THE SHORE

It was time to share her feelings about Tim — with the other woman in his life.

SALLY dug her hands into the cool sand, enjoying the sensation as it slipped slowly through her fingers. She rested her chin on her knees and gazed back along the beach.

The couple, coming steadily nearer, from the direction of the promenade, were arm in arm, carrying their shoes and kicking at the gentle spray as it rolled towards the shore. She couldn't yet see their faces, but a small knot of fear was growing inside her. She knew exactly who they were.

Behind her, from the roadside, a tall stone lamp snapped a beam of light across the sands; then another and another, as the promenade prepared itself for the night ahead. Somewhere a pub door swung open, releasing a brief burst of merriment into the air.

Sally looked again in the direction of the advancing figures. They were coming towards *her*, as she sat in the deepening gloom, outwith the brightness of the lamp.

Earlier, she'd sat alone in the flat, watching the clock and listening for the sound of Tim's key in the lock. In vain she tried to concentrate on other things, switching on the television and staring blindly at the flashing images on the screen, until at last she could stand the waiting no longer.

And so she'd jumped in her car and driven to the beach, intending to watch the sun go down over the sea, but when she'd seen Tim's head above the early evening strollers, she hadn't been surprised. In her heart she'd known that this was where he'd come tonight.

Tim loved it here.

She'd noticed how a stroll along the beach could calm him in times of stress, fill him with hope in times of despair.

Sitting in the shelter of his arms, together they'd watched the seasons change.

She dreaded the day when she would sit alone, because her heart ached for fear of losing him.

And so she'd walked along the beach, and sat on the sand and waited. She knew if they came, that they'd sit right there, where the wide circle of steps swept out on to the beach, bright now in the rays of the lamp.

From here she'd watch, because she'd never seen them together before, and she needed to see how it was between them — before tomorrow.

Hopefully, they wouldn't see her. She could tell they weren't engaged in idle conversation, casting their eyes about to take in the twilight view. Lost in a deep exchange of feelings and emotions, their eyes saw no farther than each other.

She seemed an earnest young woman, using her hands to emphasise her words, as her long blonde hair echoed every movement of her head.

Tim sauntered beside her, a figure of stability, turning towards her now and then.

Sally could only imagine the warmth in his eyes, the gentle creases round his mouth as he smiled. Tonight his smiles were for the girl.

Now they were level with the steps. Sally held her breath, remembering the times when she and Tim had strolled along the beach as far as this point, a natural resting place to stop and talk, because nothing was simple and there was so much to talk about.

Closing her eyes, she suddenly wished she were somewhere else — anywhere but here, in the lingering stillness of an early summer evening, watching Tim take the girl's hand and lead her to a spot in the lamplight where they could talk.

She would see now how it was when they were together. She could sense the bond which secured them — a father and daughter, safe in the knowledge that their love needed no justification, while she hid and skulked in shadows, the other woman, the villain of the story.

IN the beginning she'd been the secretary, attractive and confident, while Tim, although the boss, had been the more vulnerable — the victim of a loveless marriage. On the face of it the old familiar tale of triangles and infidelity.

But only on the face of it . . . "I won't have an affair with you," Sally had told him seriously one lazy afternoon snatched from the turmoil of the days.

He'd nodded slowly. "I know," was all he'd said.

And yet, just to be there with him, sharing his company in a quiet, country pub, had made her feel that the betrayal was already complete.

Still it made no sense. How could it be so wrong to love someone; to sometimes touch and sometimes laugh and sometimes simply walk and talk? How could these things be wrong — even though that person belonged to someone else?

She'd found no answer in her own childhood days, so secure and loving and free from complication; no answer in the knowing winks of friends and colleagues; no answer anywhere . . .

Until the day they'd strolled along the beach and rested on the steps, just beyond the lamp's bright rays, and Tim had said, "I'm leaving her, Sally. It's sheer madness to struggle through another day."

Sally had gazed across the beach, watching the waves as they foamed towards the shore.

"Now we have a choice." His voice had been husky and low. "Either I find myself a flat somewhere — or I come to you."

Was it so very wrong that her heart had sung for joy at his words? Did her decision that day condemn her for ever in the eyes of the world — or merely in the eyes of a young girl with sun-kissed hair and an earnest disposition?

"No." Sally found herself saying the word aloud as she looked once more towards the couple on the steps. Two years was long enough. Now she knew why she'd come here to wait for them. The hiding was over.

Slowly she walked towards them, but they were too preoccupied with each other to notice her. Even when she stood beside them, it was several seconds before they seemed to sense her presence, and their heads turned.

"Sally!" Tim leapt to his feet.

"I didn't follow you," Sally said shakily, looking at the girl. "I was sitting over there on the sand. I thought perhaps it was time we met."

The girl met her gaze.

"Sally . . . this is my daughter, Helen," Tim said helplessly.

"Hello, Helen . . ." Sally held out her hand. "It's good to meet you at last."

The girl studied Sally for a moment, then jumped from the steps and began to walk back along the beach.

Tim made to follow his daughter, but Sally caught his arm.

"Let me try, Tim. Please," she pleaded. He relaxed, nodding his head and smiling encouragement.

"Helen . . ." Sally shouted, stumbling over the uneven surface after her. The girl was running, kicking her bare feet in the sand. "Helen . . . You can't pretend I don't exist."

At that Helen stopped and turned round. "I know you exist all right," she hissed, as Sally struggled towards her. "I knew before Mum did. I just wish you didn't exist — then everything could be like it used to be."

"We can't turn back the clock, Helen."

Helen raised her eyes and spread her arms dramatically. "Oh, spare me the clichés. I've heard them all from Dad. It's sad, but sometimes people don't get it right first time round."

She kicked fiercely at the sand. "But who's it sad for, that's what I want to know? It's not sad for you, or for Dad."

"Isn't it? How can you be so sure about that?"

"I'm sure!" Her voice was rising to a shriek. "You had a choice, didn't you? Even Mum had a choice. She could have done something, fought to keep Dad but she didn't.

"She just sat back and let you take him. She didn't even seem to care about the divorce.

"And now even she's found someone else — someone called Dave and she keeps asking me if I like him. As if it matters whether I like him or not!

135

And don't tell me my dad still loves me. I know that, too."

Sally had a growing feeling there was nothing she could tell this young woman that she didn't already know. There was no way through the armour of her resentment, nothing that could even begin to justify the pain she'd suffered and the tears she'd shed.

How could she ask the girl's forgiveness? How could she say, "Please forgive me, Helen. I've taken your dad away from your home. I've shattered your cosy normality and now you have to get to know a man called Dave.

"But you must try to understand, because I need you to, and your dad needs you to — before tomorrow . . ."

HAVE you ever been married?" Helen's sudden question jarred through her thoughts.

"No, I haven't."

"Why not? You're quite pretty and you're exactly double my age. Hey, thirty-four's a bit ancient to be single, isn't it?" Helen was walking across the wet sand, her fingers tucked casually into the pockets of her baggy jeans.

"There's been no-one I've wanted to spend my life with — until now."

"So why couldn't you find someone of your own? Why did you have to steal another woman's husband? Why did you have to steal my dad?"

Sally shivered.

"It wasn't quite the way you think."

"He came to *you*, didn't he? Is that it? Well, you could have stopped him, if you'd wanted to."

"No. I couldn't. I . . ."

"Don't tell me — let me guess. This thing's bigger than both of you. Right?"

"Well, that's one way of putting it." Sally hid a grim smile. Helen had a way of stripping every sentiment to the bone. She was a formidable adversary.

"I don't blame you for loving him." The girl was looking back at the lonely figure on the steps. Then she turned to Sally, tilting her head and narrowing her eyes.

"I call you 'that woman'," she goaded. "Sometimes I call you 'the old bat'. I write things about you, too. If you read my diary, it would make your hair curl."

"It's a pity you didn't bring it with you." Sally was fighting for control. The tears were stinging her eyes, but she couldn't weaken now. She'd made this happen.

She could have stayed in the shadows and watched, then slunk away into the night, still "the other woman", the guilty one. But she'd chosen to step into the light, and there was no going back.

"I didn't need to bring it. I know it off by heart." Helen had walked a few more paces towards the sea, allowing the gentle swell to lap around her ankles and dampen her jeans.

The beach was in darkness now, only the promenade and the steps remained illuminated.

"I've got a boyfriend." She gave Sally a sideways look, her face half-covered by her long hair. "His name's Mark and he's eighteen, a year older than me. He's incredibly good-looking. If someone stole Mark from me, I'd tear her heart out."

Sally stood, just beyond the reach of the sea. The girl was looking down, watching the dark, wet patch creep up her jeans.

"That's because you love him," Sally said softly. "If someone stole your dad from me, I'd tear her heart out, too."

Helen laughed harshly. "Well, that's great — coming from you." A sly smile touched her lips. "What if I stole him back from you?

"He loves me, too, you know. I've been quite brave . . . considering. I could stop being brave. I could steal him from you if I wanted to. What would you do then?"

Sally met the girl's eyes. She was trembling inside, but her voice was clear and cool.

"I'd tear your heart out," she said quietly.

She saw the smile fade, but the eyes didn't waver. It was as though a cloud of doubt had cast its shadow across the young girl's face.

"That's how I feel about Mark." Her voice was soft and uncertain. "I'd never let him go without a fight. He makes me feel like I'm burning inside."

She cast her eyes upwards, and Sally saw a single tear slide gently down her cheek. Then she was walking, back towards the steps.

SALLY watched the slim, retreating figure, saw her pause and slowly turn. "About . . . tomorrow . . ." The shrill, young voice drifted across the sands.

"Yes? What about tomorrow, Helen?"

"I'm not taking back anything I've said. And I'm going to make quite sure *I* get it right *first* time round. But . . . I might come to the wedding if . . . if I can bring Mark."

"Of course you can."

"Fine." She turned and strode up the beach to join her father, grabbing her shoes from the bottom step.

"Come on, Dad. You'd better take me home." She took the steps two at a time, then sauntered off along the promenade, swinging her shoes.

"Will you come back here for me, Tim?" Sally called across the beach. "I'd like to stay for a while longer." Tim nodded and smiled.

She watched him catch up with his daughter and take her arm, then she looked up at the bright, clear moon and took a deep, contented breath.

There was someone out there she'd never even seen, someone who had taught a young woman how to love, and she had a feeling she owed him more than he would ever know.

"Thanks, Mark," she whispered into the darkness, "Thank you so very much." ■

Through

by Sally Woods

138

Gemma's Eyes

Their problems seemed terribly complicated — until her daughter showed her how simple the solution could be.

ROSEMARY flicked through the morning post, automatically setting aside the few buff-coloured envelopes which she guessed were bills. There were plenty of letters this morning — what a nice surprise.

She sat down at the kitchen table to examine the three handwritten envelopes — these looked much more interesting than the bills. There was no end of those at the moment. The worst of it was, there was never enough money to cover them.

And as if that wasn't bad enough, there were the constant rows between her and Andy because of the shortage of cash.

"Why do we have to stay in a house we can't afford," Andy had shouted the previous night, "when my parents' cottage is lying empty? All it needs is a few repairs and a lick of paint!"

That cottage was fine for holidays — but to live in it and make it their home? That was another question altogether.

Then there was Andy's idea of opening a shop in what was virtually the cottage's front parlour. It all seemed such a gamble . . .

OK, there were advantages — the cottage was situated close to the beach and near to a school, and there were plenty of other houses nearby. Also, Andy felt the shop would be popular because there wasn't a supermarket within a 20-mile radius. Even so, to give up all they had . . .

"It would be *better* than what we have now!" Andy had argued, frustrated and furious.

"Have you any idea what it's like, working at a job you hate — always struggling for more sales, more commission? Someone pushing you all the time to try harder . . . Well, I'm sick of it!"

"Something better will turn up, Andy," she had ventured, trying to be understanding.

"Will it? You've been saying that for the past two years, Rosemary!"

He was right, of course. Ever since the small industrial firm, of which he'd been manager, had folded, she'd been doing her utmost to boost his confidence by saying something would turn up soon.

But to give up their lovely house to live in a run-down cottage? That was a lot to ask.

"I could leave the bakery — find a full-time job," she'd suggested, desperately trying to find a way round the problem.

Andy had shaken his head in exasperation. "Where? You'll be lucky round here. Anyway, you said yourself you don't want to work full-time, and have Gemma coming home from school to an empty house."

"Gemma's almost twelve years old. She's not a baby any more."

He gave her a long look then, and she had to turn away to prevent him from seeing the tears that had suddenly welled up in her eyes. She blinked rapidly.

Strange, how the memory of her own childhood had a way of confronting her every now and then.

"If we sold this place, and paid our mortgage, we should have enough left to stock a general shop —"

"You're always on about this shop, Andy!" she broke in. "What do we know about running a shop?"

"We could manage, I know we could. You have the bakery experience and we'd be living right on the premises — always one of us there for Gemma coming home."

Gemma, who'd been sitting there quietly as usual during these frequent arguments, suddenly spoke up. "I could help in the shop after school," she said, "and at weekends . . ."

140

"That's another thing," Rosemary flared. "If we moved away from here, Gemma would miss all her friends."

"That's OK, Mum, I'll soon be changing schools, anyway, and making new friends. In any case, it would be worth it just to —" Abruptly she stopped talking, and hung her head.

The thick, auburn hair swung forward to hide her face from them. Gemma hated these rows and Rosemary guessed what her young daughter had been about to say — that anything would be worth it to have her parents stop rowing.

But, Rosemary reflected, Gemma was too young to possibly imagine the heart-searching involved in such a decision. To her, it would seem an adventure.

PUSHING her unhappy thoughts aside, Rosemary turned her attention to the three envelopes in her hand.

One was addressed to her and Andy, in a childish hand that was very familiar. Gemma! Quickly she glanced at the other two envelopes, her eyes scanning the handwriting — one was for her, the other for Andy — but the handwriting, on both, was unfamiliar.

"Oh no!" she exclaimed, pulling out a greetings card from the envelope. It was an anniversary card! Inside was a sweet, flowing verse, and beneath it Gemma had written, *To Mum and Dad. I love you both very much, Gemma.*

There were hugs and kisses under Gemma's signature. Of course, it was their 15th wedding anniversary. With a sinking feeling in her heart, she realised she'd forgotten.

141

How sweet of Gemma to remember. But then she kept a little notebook in which she kept a record of all her friends' and family birthdays and special dates.

Rosemary picked up the second envelope — the one addressed to herself. Had Andy remembered to send *her* a card? It wasn't his handwriting. In fact, she didn't recognise the writing at all. It was all squiggles and curls.

She studied the card inside. *To my darling wife on our anniversary.* Then she opened it and stared in puzzlement at Andy's signature, followed by a row of kisses.

This wasn't how Andy signed his name — but it did look as if someone might have tried to copy it.

Slowly, Rosemary picked up the third and last envelope — the one for Andy. This time the name and address were printed. She held it up to the light — definitely another card!

She examined the two cards she'd opened more closely. With the lopsided hugs and the wavy row of kisses, it was obvious they had come from Gemma, even though she had done her best to forge Andy's signature. Oh, Gemma . . .

Then Rosemary was crying softly. The tears ran down her cheeks and fell on the cards she was holding. She could remember doing something similar herself when she was a little girl, when she'd been worried about her own parents' never-ending rows.

THAT other little girl had left notes all over the place — under her mother's pillow — in her father's pockets, everywhere she could think of. *I love you, Daddy, from Mummy. I love you, Mummy, from Daddy.* She smiled, a sad little smile, at the innocence of childhood.

For, alas, the message behind her notes had gone unheeded and Rosemary's father had finally left.

Her mother had gone out to work full time, and from then, until she left school, Rosemary had returned home every day to a lonely, empty house.

But worse than that — somehow her father had become lost to her altogether, and her mother had turned into a bitter stranger with whom she was unable to communicate.

Brushing away her tears, she looked again at the envelope bearing Andy's name. It wasn't hard to guess that Gemma had sent this one, too. She knew if she opened it and looked inside, it would say: *From Rosemary,* followed by a row of kisses.

Poor Gemma — what they must have put the child through! This was her way of trying to prevent her parents' rows — by having each think they still loved the other, just as Rosemary, herself, had tried to do all those years ago.

What were they going to do? Correction — what was *she* going to do?

Crying was getting her nowhere. She dried her eyes on a tissue.

142

Without a moment's more hesitation, she rang the bakery to tell them she was sorry but she wouldn't be in today.

Then she displayed the two cards she had opened on the mantelpiece. Andy's card she propped unopened, against a vase.

This was Andy's morning for compiling orders in the office. She would ask him to go along with the pretence of Gemma's cards. Then separately, they would thank her for sending a card, confessing they'd completely forgotten it was their anniversary. At least that part of it would be true. Deep down, she and Andy still loved each other, didn't they?

But there was something else she must tell Andy. Something she couldn't wait to tell him. The cottage, the shop — all of it! She would give it a go. Together they would make it work. The most important thing was all being together.

Looking round her lovely home she felt a small pang for what they'd be leaving but — after all — it was just a house . . .

Suddenly, she felt fired by a great sense of challenge and excitement. She and Andy opening their own business; getting the cottage into shape; turning it into a permanent home. She would be able to provide home-made cakes and bread for their shop and they'd all pull together.

Suddenly memories she'd been suppressing surged back: the holidays they'd spent in the cottage; long, sunny days on the beach; barbecues in the evenings. There would be time for all of that as well. They would *make* time.

But for now, there was so much to do here — a cake to bake, and a meal to prepare for the little celebration dinner she was already planning for that evening. There would be just the three of them — she and Andy, and their very special daughter. ■

Employing a
housekeeper
had seemed like
a good idea —
but this one
appeared to be
making a clean
sweep of their
whole lives!

"A PERFECT TREASURE!"

by Elizabeth Drummond

TODAY, what Susan noticed first was the lock — the front door lock. For as long as she could remember, it had been obstinate, requiring a certain sequence of pushes and releases before the mechanism yielded and the door would jerk reluctantly open, protesting creakily. Not today, though!

Today, her key slid snugly into place and turned smoothly, and the

144

door swung back silently. Susan shivered, and stepped into the front hall.

It was, as she expected, immaculate. Everything shone, as she had known it would — the small, half-moon table, gleaming, with her mother's cherished brass kettle glowing between the two shining candlesticks, all reflected in the long mirror, also highly polished.

She could smell the polish, and there was another fragrance, too, tonight. What was it?

Ah, yes, that was what was different — the pot-pourri, in the shallow, wooden bowl that usually held fruit in the dining-room.

So what had Mrs M. done with the fruit? Cautiously, she peered round the dining-room door.

She might have known! The basket she and Jeffrey had brought back from their Italian honeymoon was now crowned with a golden pyramid of oranges, apples and bananas. It looked good.

No, to be honest, it looked lovely — appetising and enticing — and very much better than the bowl, she could see that.

With the now-familiar sensation of tightness in her chest, Susan hung up her coat and went into the kitchen.

She was not aware of having clenched her fists until, reaching for the kettle, she had to force open her hand; mildly surprised, she examined her palms, each with four, angry, half-moon indentations.

Stress, she supposed — or Mrs M.!

Jeffrey would say she was being neurotic, of course. Not that she would ever find the words to explain the problem — to Jeffrey or anyone else.

There, she'd used the word — *problem!* She said it out loud, as she shook instant coffee into a mug. *"Problem!* I have a *problem!"*

If she ever did say that — Jeffrey — always supposing he wasn't too busy to listen — would want to know what it was, and she couldn't imagine telling him.

"Mrs M.," she said now, to the kettle. *"Mrs M.'s my problem!"* But no-one would believe her.

IT had been Jeffrey who had found Mrs M. after all. Now that Oliver and Annabel were both at school, it was time for Susan to resume her interrupted career.

At least, that was how they both put it. Before the children came along, she had worked in an art gallery, just a small one, but well thought of.

She had talked of returning one day, but it had closed, quietly and sadly, one Bank Holiday weekend, and she'd never heard what had happened to Bette, who'd run it.

Susan had gone on to find a new job, in a rather exclusive dress shop, the kind that believed that one garment and a vase of flowers was adequate window-dressing.

"I don't want an assistant," Meg, the proprietor, had told her. "An
145

adviser, that's what I'm looking for. To advise the customers, dear."

But it didn't seem any different from the art gallery, really, where her job, after all, was to sell pictures. She'd had commission there, too.

Still, it was a toe on the ladder, Jeffrey said. He didn't want to stifle *his* wife by insisting that she stayed at home, and he was quite ready to shoulder his share of the chores in order to free her to go back to the real world.

SO Susan started her job, her mother caring for the children after school, and Jeffrey occasionally washing up or emptying the waste-paper bin.

Susan cooked, cleaned, washed, ironed, made packed lunches, found lost school-books and battled with a rising tide of exhaustion and irritation.

Jeffrey did insist, however, on doing the shopping. She had to write a list for him, in the order things were to be found at the local supermarket, although he often lost it or simply ignored it.

It really would have been simpler to go herself and let *him* clean the bath or wash the kitchen floor. But he always insisted, "No, I said I'd do my share. It's only right."

But it definitely wasn't enough — even Jeffrey could see that.

And, incredibly, it was at the supermarket that he found Mrs M.

Mrs M. was in the same queue at the checkout. Jeffrey had returned triumphant that night, with the wrong kind of bacon and without the loo rolls, of which they had been in imminent need, but with an announcement.

The household help problem was solved! He'd got into conversation with the woman behind him in the queue. There had been some kind of hold up at the check-out. ("A hold up, Daddy?" Oliver had squealed excitedly, but Jeffrey paid no attention.) and everybody got talking to one another, well grumbling, really!

"This woman behind me said she should have known better than come in at that time," he'd said, unpacking groceries all over the kitchen table which Susan had just cleared for the children's supper.

"And I happened to say that we couldn't shop at any other time because you had a little job now. She said she was looking for a part-time job, herself, and, well, there you are. I've arranged for her to come round and see us on Saturday."

"But, what's she like?"

"Oh, you'll find her ideal, honestly, darling, just the job. I'm sure she'll fit the bill."

And Mrs M. ("It's Matthews, dear, but just call me Mrs M.") had indeed seemed to fit the bill.

She was younger than Susan had expected, neat but fairly ordinary in appearance with a cold handshake and a business-like way of asking and answering all the right questions.

When they'd agreed hours and money, she'd smiled and said briskly, "Well, that's it then. I'll see you right."

CRADLING her mug of coffee, Susan sat at the kitchen table and pondered. When had things started to go wrong? Not the first week, or even the second.

What a joy it had been to return, after rather a boring day at the boutique, to a spotless, well-ordered home. She had gradually begun to relax and there had been time again for the children, time at the weekends to do things together as a family.

One day, Mrs M. picked flowers from the garden and arranged them, very professionally it seemed to Susan, in a nice glass vase that she had found in a cupboard.

She'd even left her a note, typed out on Annabel's toy typewriter: *Hope it was all right to do the flowers.* Susan had smiled, and scribbled underneath, *Of course. Thanks.*

That was a mistake, she saw that now. So, if things were going wrong, it was really her own fault. Mrs M. had gained a toe in the door and there was no stopping her.

She tidied out the kitchen cupboards and rearranged them. Well, it made more sense to have tea, coffee, sugar and mugs all together near the kettle.

Jeffrey heartily approved. "Wonderful woman," he said. He was having staffing problems of his own at the office, with the receptionist being pregnant and leaving soon, and no likely replacement on the horizon.

Mrs M. washed the downstairs curtains and hung the dining-room ones in the living-room, and the living-room ones in the dining-room and, at a stroke, made both rooms look like Habitat showpieces.

Thought you might like a change, her note had said on that occasion.

"Lucky you!" Susan's friends enthused when they came round for supper — there was time to entertain again, now that Mrs M. was organising and cleaning everything.

Susan just smiled, and tried to feel at home.

Mrs M. even found space in the cupboard at the back door for the clutter of children's wellingtons, sandals and slippers that had provided an obstacle course for unwary visitors.

She made little notices to mark where everything should go, and Oliver and Annabel, surprisingly, actually began to remember to tidy their discarded footwear away.

"Amazing," Susan's mother said approvingly. Susan felt it was unnatural, herself. She worried that the children would develop complexes and be even more difficult as teenagers than she already expected them to be.

She'd have liked to discuss it with Jeffrey, but he was increasingly preoccupied with the impending crisis at work. Anyway, as far as Mrs M. was concerned, he was always understandably smug, having discovered her in the first place.

And it *was* amazing — of course it was. But, little by little, it was also rather disturbing.

Susan sipped her coffee, arguing with herself. What on earth was the matter with her?

She had a loving husband, two delightful children, a career (well, all right then, a job, but that was more than lots of people had), a cleaning lady who was honest and reliable, and a comfortable home.

She put down her mug. "No, I haven't," she said aloud. "Because I don't feel at home here any more!"

SHE looked round the kitchen. The spices in the rack were now arranged in order of size, because that's how Mrs M. had put them — but they used to be set out alphabetically.

The shelf of saucepans, gleaming, were similarly marshalled — but Susan had always kept the two most in use on the cooker.

The kitchen table had been placed meticulously in the middle of the floor, so that it no longer blocked access to the washing machine — but sitting here she could no longer see out of the window. And, anyway, the window-sill had an array of geraniums donated by her perfect household help.

Just cuttings from my own plants, her typed note had read. *Don't worry about them. I'll keep an eye on them and see them right.*

That was the problem in a nutshell. Mrs M. was so determined to "see everything right" — the geraniums, the saucepans, the children's wellingtons, the front hall, everything — that Susan felt like a visitor in her own house, the house that used to be her home.

She was clenching her fists again. It was time for action — *now* before Jeffrey came home and while the children were still with her mother.

First, she put her mug on the draining-board, and did not wash it. Next, she tipped the spices from the spice rack and rearranged them alphabetically.

The geraniums she thrust out of doors, the table she dragged back against the washing machine, and she'd just finished with the saucepans when Jeffrey came in.

"What the —" he began, and then, seeing her flushed and defiant face, "— darling?"

Susan burst into tears.

It took some time to convince him, as she'd known it would. "She *is* perfect, of course she is," she assured him. "It *was* wonderful of you to find her, really it was.

"It's just that she's *too* perfect for me, that's all. And . . . and . . ." As a new burst of illumination washed over her, "I . . . I don't really care for that job, anyway, Jeffrey. To be honest, it's frightfully boring . . ."

"Well, why on earth didn't you *say*?"

Susan couldn't blame him for feeling annoyed. "I've only just discovered it for myself," she confessed.

"Would it mess things up awfully if I gave it up? And stayed at home — at least until the children are a little bigger?"

"And give Mrs M. notice, you mean?" His eyebrows shot up.

Susan shivered. "Whatever can we say to her? I mean, she's perfect, isn't she?"

"We'll just say you've decided to stay at home," Jeffrey said thoughtfully, "or — wait a bit — I've got it!"

And, with that, Susan had to be content.

SOME time later — after bidding goodbye to Meg and the boutique and, apologetically, to Mrs M. — Susan called in at Jeffrey's office.

The new receptionist was typing busily. She looked up, eyebrows raised in enquiry.

Susan stopped dead. It was — it couldn't be — it *was!* Elegantly slim, her hair now styled much more becomingly, thin fingers poised over the keyboard . . .

"Good morning!" Mrs M. smiled warmly at Susan.

"Mrs M.!" Susan gasped.

Mrs M. nodded and smiled again.

"Makes a nice change from housework, and there's lots to do. I used to work in an office, you know."

"I didn't know," Susan eventually said faintly. "My husband —"

"Yes, when I heard you didn't need me any more *and* he let slip about this vacancy here — well . . ."

"I see." Susan nodded. "How — how nice for you. And for him," she added hastily. "He didn't actually tell me, you see."

"No?" Mrs M. seemed genuinely surprised. "I expect he wanted to surprise you. Suits me very well, I must say. And I must say —" Her glance encompassed the filing cabinets, bookshelves, the cupboards by the window, "—nobody's put this place straight for a very long time. But I'll see them right."

There was a pot of geraniums on her desk that Susan was sure hadn't been there before. "I'm sure you will," Susan agreed fervently. "I have no doubt of that at all!" ∎

To Erin, With

Like her memories, her father's gift was one she would treasure for ever . . .

A S I draw back the pretty floral curtains, a pink and golden day greets me warmly.

The gardens below sparkle with glistening dew, giving them a new-washed look, and I notice that the buds on the trees are unfurling; that brave, green shoots are poking tentatively through the earth, with the promise of beauty to come.

There is new life all around me and it makes me smile in knowledge and anticipation.

Happily, I breathe in the fresh, cool, morning air, trying to steady the erratic thump of my heart, but it's no use. Excitement simply courses through me.

Not long now . . .

*   *   *   *

When Vivien and Dennis Alcott first came into my life, I was nine years old. They turned up at the orphanage one day and almost before I knew it, they'd officially adopted me.

From there on, I knew only great love and a deep sense of security, although these earlier years had left their mark by knocking all the confidence out of me.

I had despaired of anyone ever loving me, for I had been one of those rather plain, awkward, freckled, skinny kids who had constantly found herself passed over by prospective parents in favour of the younger, beautiful, pink and white kids; the ones with blond curls or dark, glossy locks and engaging grins.

Each rejection drew me deeper into the private world I shared with no-one.

"Be a good girl for the Alcotts, Erin," Matron said to me the day I went to live with them. She needn't have worried.

There was a desperation in me to belong somewhere; to be part of a loving family, that even now I find difficult to put into words.

Lifting my face to hers, I remember replying earnestly, "I will, Matron. I promise."

And, to my complete surprise, her eyes filled with tears as she drew me close to her. I could feel her heart beating as she murmured, "You're a dear child, you know, Erin. I'll miss you very much."

150

Love

by
Josefine
Beaumont

Then, holding me at arm's length, she added, "You mean a lot to me, dear, and maybe I shouldn't say this . . . but you've always been one of my favourite children."

I hugged her tightly. Her words are still in my heart even now after all these years.

THERE was none of the initial awkwardness with the Alcotts that I had feared there might be.

They took me into their home, their lives, and into their hearts. From day one I was *their* daughter.

"Well, for a start, you won't need that thing any more," Vivien told me, discarding the cheap, brown cardboard suitcase, which held my meagre possessions. I remember her words filling me with hope and elation.

Vivien Alcott was a large, jolly, vivacious woman with smooth, creamy skin and big brown eyes that danced with the sheer joy of life.

Her size meant she was forced to wear voluminous dresses she laughingly called her "Bedouin tents". She had a passion for ridiculous

151

hats and an abundance of love and time for me.

Dennis Alcott was himself, a big, bulky man — six foot tall in his socks. He was barrel-chested with enormous hands and feet — like malt shovels — and a ready smile always played about his lips.

His passion was gardening — roses in particular, which he grew in abundance.

Every evening, from late spring onwards, found him in the garden, tending to his precious roses which he grew in every hue and shade you could think of.

Often in the summer, I joined him, pottering about the flower beds, finding peace and contentment myself just be being there with him amidst the profusion and perfume of his prize roses.

Over the years, I came to love them both dearly. They were wonderful people and totally devoted to each other. He would affectionately call her "lass," while she referred to him as "dear" with equal tenderness.

There was no doubt they had something special together.

"We met at sixteen and were married at eighteen," Vivien confided in me, one night when we were gathered around the fire.

Her knitting needles were clicking furiously together and her chin was wobbling, at the mere mention of their teenage love. The fond memory had obviously struck a chord in her heart.

"And we've been happy ever since," Dennis reminded her, lowering his newspaper, his eyes twinkling as the colour tinged her face until it resembled a rose as red as those that grew in the back garden.

"Isn't that so, lass?" He quirked an eyebrow.

"Silly man!" she muttered fondly, her face a picture of delight.

"Mind," he winked at me, "she's not above laying the rolling-pin across my ear if I step out of line!"

"I've never heard such nonsense in all my days!" she blustered, as I stifled a giggle. "You should be ashamed of yourself, Dennis Alcott! You'll scare the child half to death."

Then turning to me, she said, "Take no notice of him, Erin."

On the contrary, I grew used to their bantering over the months because he teased her unmercifully, and she loved every minute of it. I loved every minute of it, too. Just as I loved the plentiful hugs and kisses this demonstrative couple showered upon me.

All my short life I had been starved of love and affection — those fundamental joys — and now thanks to these two good people, I had an abundance of them.

THUS my life took on a new pattern, and the months slipped into years, each of them blissfully happy and fulfilled.

But there was one time when I remember feeling less than happy. I must have been about 11 years old when Mum caught me staring dolefully at my reflection in the mirror.

"What's the matter, Erin?" she asked softly.

I turned to her and asked, "Why am I plain, Mum?"

"Plain?" She turned red. "Rubbish! You're not plain. What makes you think a thing like that, for goodness' sake?"

Turning back to the mirror, I sighed wistfully.

"I wish I had curly hair like Sue Robinson in my class. She's so pretty."

"And so are you, my lovely," she replied quickly. "You want curls?" Her eyes danced. "Then curls you shall have!"

And from then on, each night, she would sit patiently rag rollering my hair, and the following morning I'd skip along the road to school, my curls dancing around my shoulders.

And that's about as far as being unhappy ever went.

At school, I worked hard for three reasons: obviously, I wanted to please Mum and Dad; secondly because I actually enjoyed learning and studying; and lastly because I needed good grades to get into nursing college.

In the end my dedication paid off when I was accepted for the nursing course I wanted so much.

But the worst part of it all for me was the parting with my parents. They came to the railway station with me and I could see the strained look on Dad's face as he tried desperately to hide his sorrow. And I couldn't help noticing the way Mum's chin was wobbling alarmingly.

My heart ached for them.

The night before I left, they had come into my bedroom where I was busy packing and after a lot of humming and hawing, hesitantly, Dad had asked, "Have you ever wondered about your . . . your real parents, lass?"

I'd stared at him, swallowed hard and replied truthfully, "Not much. Not for years now, Dad. I used to when I was little . . ."

They'd exchanged uncertain glances and, clearing his throat, Dad had said, "The thing is, love, if you want to try to trace them we'll understand. It's maybe not what we'd want," he added quickly, "but it's your life and we'd understand if you . . ."

"I don't want that," I'd replied gently. "*You're* my parents. You brought me up and I love you both. Nothing else matters."

"You're not just saying that to spare our feelings, are you, dear?" Mum had asked anxiously, reaching for Dad's hand. They' looked so worried!

153

"No, I'm not." I'd shaken my head, at the same time putting my arms round them both.

My emphatic reply had seemed to give them some comfort.

"Well, that's all right then." Dad had stood up, smiling his lopsided smile.

It had made me realise that they'd loved and needed me as much as I had loved them. And now I was leaving.

WRITE often," Mum had pleaded, tearfully.

"And phone us, lass." Dad's voice had been gruff with emotion. "Reverse the charges, mind."

"I will," I'd promised.

"See that you eat properly now and remember to have plenty of fresh fruit," Mum had reminded me, dabbing her eyes.

"And I'll make sure I'm wearing nice, clean underwear," I'd chimed in, grinning, "in case a bus knocks me down and I have to go to hospital!"

My silly quip had lightened the moment and we'd all laughed.

"The train's here." Dad had nodded in the direction of the Inter-city express as it pulled into the station. After he'd heaved my luggage into the compartment and hoisted it on to the rack, we'd been left standing looking at each other.

Suddenly, Dad had held his arms open wide.

"Come here, lass." His eyes had been filled with tears and that had set me off.

I'd thrown myself into his arms, burying my face in his shoulder. I'd wanted to thank him, thank both of them for choosing *me* at the orphanage, but my throat was too full for words.

Doors had slammed, a whistle had blown. Briefly I'd been enveloped in Mum's ample arms, before scrambling on to the train at the last minute.

I'd hung out of the window, waving frantically as the train pulled away from the platform until they were almost out of sight.

My last mental picture is of them huddled together for comfort and reassurance.

One day I hoped I would be fortunate enough to find that kind of love and closeness in a relationship.

As the train had rounded the bend, I'd noticed a flutter of white and in that last brief glimpse, I'm sure I'd seen Dad wipe his eyes with his handkerchief.

Sinking back in my seat, oblivious to the stares of the other passengers, I'd allowed the tears to stream, unchecked, down my face . . .

I never saw my father alive again.

There are all kinds of nightmares. Some we remember, others we forget. Some creep up on us in sleep, others visit us in the cold light of day.

My worst nightmare still concerns the unexpected phone call I received in the small, dark hours. I'll never forget the sound of Mum's voice. I knew I was listening to the sound of her tears.

I had never heard her cry before — just as I have never known such fear.

Several things made that night so awful, so memorable — the tension I felt as my hand gripped the phone, the way the cold seeped through my nightdress . . .

And the fact that, in the end, I arrived home too late.

In my naiveté, I had thought that I would be a comfort to Mum, but, in fact she ended up comforting me. I was inconsolable for days.

Three weeks later, I went back to college, much against my will, but Mum had insisted.

"Your dad loved you very much," she had told me gently, "and he was so proud of you, dear. It's time you carried on with your life. It's what he would have wanted you to do."

Two months later, she phoned me one Wednesday night as usual and her voice sounded bright, almost like it used to be.

I tried to match her cheerfulness.

"You will be home, won't you, dear — at the weekend?"

"Of course I will." I'd been going home every weekend since Dad's death. What's she up to? I thought.

"That's good. I'll see you on Saturday, then. Oh, Erin," I could hear laughter and tears in her voice now. "I've such a lovely surprise for you."

Gripping the receiver, I smiled to myself. "That's a coincidence, Mum, I have one for you, too!"

"You know what I think, love? You've met someone," she stated happily, sounding pleased.

"Ehm, well, yes I have actually, Mum. I've met someone, and," added, shyly, "I'd like you to meet him."

"What's he like? Is he a doctor? How did you meet?"

Then I hesitated before saying, "Well . . . he's like . . . he's sort of like Dad . . ."

For a moment there was total silence at the other end of the phone and then — "Well, dear, why don't you bring him home with you this weekend?" she asked softly.

AND so I went home with Tom at my side.

We'd met at the teaching hospital where Tom was a fourth-year medical student and where I went regularly as part of my training.

Somehow I think we'd both known almost immediately that we were destined for each other.

He was big and kind and gentle — all the qualities I had admired so much in my father.

Tom had even said to me, on our first date, "I'm going to marry you one day — as soon as I've qualified. I thought I'd better warn you!"

The colour had risen to my face and I remember giving an embarrassed laugh and saying, "Don't be silly! You don't even know me."

"As soon as I saw that cute, freckled nose," he had continued, totally unperturbed, "and that long, shining hair, I thought, that's the girl for me!"

And I'd always thought myself rather unattractive!

"You're mad," I had said, but I'd felt myself flushing with pleasure.

"Totally nuts!" he had agreed cheerfully. "But only about you."

And that was all right, because I felt the same about him. And so did my mother.

"You do like him then, Mum?" I asked her anxiously, having succeeded in getting her on her own for a minute.

"He's lovely, Erin!" Those brilliant, brown eyes positively danced in her round, happy face. "What did you expect me to say? In fact seeing as toy boys are all the range, I might just marry him myself!"

And we burst out laughing as we hugged each other close.

"So what's your surprise?" I asked, suddenly remembering. She patted my arm.

"Just wait, you'll find out after lunch," she replied mysteriously.

★ ★ ★ ★

As always Mum had done us proud by serving up a first-rate meal.

"The engagement's off!" Tom declared when he'd finished, sitting back, full and satisfied in his chair. "I'm marrying your mother instead!" He couldn't understand why Mum and I were in fits of laughter again.

"What engagement?" I wriggled my ringless finger under his nose. "I don't see a ring."

"That's only because my bank balance is pretty ropey!" he admitted.

"I'm marrying a man who's penniless," I told Mum ruefully. When I looked across at her, she was smiling.

"You won't say that when I have a practice in Harley Street!" Tom protested.

"Fat chance!" I snorted and, turning to Mum, I winked. "Are you listening to this — from a man who fainted during a gallstone operation?"

"You didn't!" Mum gasped with delight.

"Only a little faint," he muttered.

"Some doctor you'll make!" I sighed.

"Oh, it's nice to hear banter in the house again," Mum said wistfully, as I reached for her hand.

I T'S time for your surprise," she said, rising to her feet. Tom and I followed her into the kitchen and out through the back door and into the garden.

On the path she paused, and turning to me, said, "You know how your dad was mad about roses? Well, what you didn't know perhaps was that he had this dream of cultivating a new variety of rose. He worked very hard at it for years and years."

Sadness overwhelmed me.

"Oh, Mum!" I breathed, tears spilling from my eyes.

"Don't cry, Erin." She smiled, drawing me close. "Just look!"

My eyes followed her hand as she gestured fondly to where a superb, deep peach rose bush was growing in one of Dad's favourite terracotta pots.

The words would not come from my lips. I was completed choked with emotion.

Instead, I looked questioningly at Mum.

"Yes, it's your dad's very own rose," she confirmed, with a nod.

Pride and the pain of his memory threatened to overwhelm me. I felt Tom's hand in mine.

"Did he . . ." I could hardly get the words out. "Did he know he'd succeeded, Mum?"

Her eyes were shining as she assured me, thus setting my world to rights.

"Oh, yes, dear, he knew . . ." Her voice faltered.

"He registered the rose three days before he died. As from this week, it'll be on sale in all the garden centres."

A mixture of relief and gratitude filled my heart to overflowing.

His dream had come true and I was so glad.

In my opinion, no man had deserved that more than he had.

"It's beautiful," I said simply.

My heart was bursting with pride, yet at the same time, heavy with sorrow.

"Yes," Mum agreed, eyes dancing now. "And he's chosen a beautiful name, too." I looked at her inquiringly through eyes misted with tears.

"He's called it the Rose of Erin," she told me with great pride, her voice now steady and controlled.

$$\star \quad \star \quad \star \quad \star$$

Not long now. Soon Tom will come and take us home from the hospital. I strain to hear his footsteps in the corridor. I can hardly wait.

Leaning over the cot I whisper to our new son, Dennis, "We're going home soon, darling."

Blue, blue eyes look up at me and fill my heart with complete happiness and contentment.

Home to where Mum waits impatiently to spoil her first grandchild; to the house where Tom and I live, and in whose garden a father's love for his daughter lives on . . . in the shape of the Rose of Erin. ■

THE SECRET POOL

When life is fraught
  When the children are quarrelling,
When my wife walks round tight lipped and angry-eyed.
When the house smells of burning toast
And I know I will lose my temper,
I leave the house and walk down the mossy path
To the secret pool that my mother made
When my sisters and I were the quarrelling children.
Our tabby cat follows me. He too needs silence.

I remember she and my father shouting at one another.
'You can't divorce me just because I like garden gnomes!'
He hated them.
So she made her hidden place where she could heal her soul,
Unseen by her quarrelling family.
Both she and my father have gone and now it is mine.

The grass grows high. The stone boy broods.
An old man sits forever on a wooden seat.
The gnomes laugh at one another across the water.
There are flowers that dwarf them all, and water lilies.
A small breeze caresses me and I build memories.

There are silver fish scything through the water.
There are red poppies, reminders of war.
One incredible day a heron comes.
Our cat is mesmerised,
Unable to believe.
He is so large that cat must think he is not a bird.
But some monster, untouchable.
Better to lie still and pretend to be invisible.

Restored, cat and I return up the mossy path.
ready to face the day and whatever it brings.
I have found my much needed peace.
The children are quiet, finishing their breakfast.
I tell them of Puss and the heron, so close to one another.
Sharing my peaceful moments. They laugh.
I kiss my wife and thank my mother
For the inspiration from her secret garden.

Joyce Stranger

Inspired by an illustration by Mark Viney

AS MIDNIGHT

by Hazel Shaw

Ivy should
have been
celebrating the
New Year's
imminent
arrival —
not worrying
about dear old
Tom's angry
departure!

DRAWS NEAR...

IVY stood by the window, peering anxiously into the evening dimness. It was after ten o'clock and Tom still hadn't come home.

If only she hadn't lost her temper with him! If only she hadn't shouted like that. He'd always hated shouting.

She'd had hours to regret their silly disagreement. In her 70s, she should have been old enough to know better! Anyway, it had been tea-time when Tom had rushed out into the icy cold of the last day of the old year.

Her anger had died in the still of the empty house. In its place came the realisation of what her ill-temper was really about.

It wasn't the mess he'd made in the kitchen, nor the fact that he'd helped himself to the last of the turkey when she'd planned to make a nice pie of it.

No, the truth was that she was unhappy and on edge because life at their new home wasn't working out as well as she'd hoped.

IT had seemed very sensible to move from the big house to a small bungalow. The housework and the garden at the old place had been too much for her for years.

Her friends had warned her she might be making a mistake. Look for somewhere nearer, they'd said.

But she'd wanted to return to the village where she'd grown up and she'd loved the bungalow, with its modern little kitchen and manageable garden. It was even close to the shops, only 15 miles from the town and their old house.

Tom hadn't been too keen on the move, but then, he didn't have to do the housework!

"We'll settle in, you'll see," she'd told him. "Just give it time."

And what had happened? They'd had a miserable, lonely Christmas, cut off from familiar friends, familiar events. Those 15 miles might as well have been 100 . . .

Now it was New Year's Eve, and Ivy had been thinking all day of happier times in friendlier places. That was really why she had blown her top when she discovered Tom in the kitchen, helping himself.

What a silly, silly thing to be angry about! He hadn't deserved the things she'd said.

Ivy opened the window and leaned out. Soft flakes of snow gilded by the yellow glow of the street light, were gently falling and melting on the ground. It wasn't heavy enough to start lying yet, thank goodness.

Oh, the silly old fool, dashing out like that with the weather so bad! He'd catch his death of cold. She'd be up half the night nursing him if he went down with one of his chests again.

But where was he? Fear clawed at Ivy's heart.

She couldn't go to their new neighbours to ask for help. She barely knew them, except by sight and the odd, "Hello, I hope you're settling in," sort of conversation.

In any case, the bungalow on the left stood silent — they'd probably gone out for the evening.

And in the house on the right there was obviously a party in progress. Lights blazed from every window and Ivy could hear muffled snatches of conversation, sounds of music, shrieks of laughter.

She could hardly knock at the door and tell them how worried she was about Tom.

No, the only thing to do was to stick it out. He'd come back when he calmed down, when he felt like coming back.

He'd always been proud, slow to forgive. But once they'd made up they would be as happy as before and all this would be forgotten.

The chiming clock struck eleven o'clock. Eleven! He'd been gone so long!

Suppose he'd had an accident? Suppose he was lying somewhere in the darkness?

If only he would come safely home, she'd never be angry with him again, not for anything.

There was no-one she could telephone, no new friend whose house he might have gone to.

IVY felt a wave of sick fear. Maybe he'd·set off for their old home, to see old friends, in spite of the fact that the only way he'd get there would be to walk.

She pictured him plodding along the main road, cars filled with party-goers whizzing by, hardly seeing him in the darkness because of his dark coat.

It would be just like the old fool to try it. He had such delusions about himself at times, because in his youth he'd been so fit and active.

Ivy closed the window, went back to the kitchen and turned on the radio. A Scots reel filled the air with its brightness and rhythm.

Ivy put the kettle on and sat down to wait for it to boil.

"I'm not going to cry," she told herself. "He's bound to be all right. He's sure to turn up none the worse."

Ivy made her tea and drank the scalding liquid slowly, half listening to the radio, trying not to face the truth that Tom had never gone off like this before.

But then, he was almost as unhappy here as she was, cut off from his old pals. No wonder he, too, had over-reacted.

Eleven-thirty. Still no sign of him, no sound.

Ivy snapped off the radio and went to get her warmest coat. She couldn't sit and do nothing any longer.

Outside the snow had begun to lie, and patches of navy-blue sky, alight with a million stars, peeped between the scudding cover of heavy grey.

It was impossible not to think of other New Years, happy times, good times, all gone for ever.

She stood by the gate, looking up and down the road, watching and waiting for a solitary figure to appear.

"Tom!" she called. "Tom!"

She felt foolish, but couldn't suppress the wild hope that he was sulking somewhere in the garden. She half expected to see him appear, safe and sound, from the shadows.

But no, he wasn't anywhere about. Either he was heading back to their old home or something awful had happened to him.

Ivy turned and went back indoors.

IT was 20 minutes to midnight when there was a ring at the doorbell. Ivy froze. This was it, the bad news. Tom had been knocked down by a car, or collapsed in the cold.

She sat rigid and silent, not wanting to move. She didn't want to hear what her caller had to say.

At last she went slowly to the door and opened it.

On the doorstep was the young husband from the house next door — and Tom was with him.

"Oh, Tom, Tom!" Ivy grabbed the furry shape and cradled him in her arms, tears of relief spilling down her cheeks.

"We thought he must be yours," the young man said. "Louise said she heard you calling for him, so I thought I'd better bring him across.

"I went out to get some logs for the fire an hour or so ago and there he was, locked in the woodshed. He was frozen.

"He's been in the house with us since then, by the fire, making friends with Mabel — that's our Persian cat."

Ivy laughed through her tears.

"The silly old thing," she said. "He had me so worried. I was sure he'd been knocked down, or run away. You've no idea the terrible things I've been imagining.

"I'd be lost without him. He's just like a human being to me — he's been a real companion since my husband died."

THE young man glanced past her into the empty house. "You're on your own!" he said. "And it's New Year's Eve! If only we'd known —"

He took her arm. "Look, you must come and join our party. I know we're probably making a lot of noise, but it's just me and Louise, my father and Louise's parents, and one or two old friends. You'll like them. Come on, it's almost midnight!"

They stood in a circle in a bright, warm, tinsel-trimmed room, singing Auld Lang Syne.

Ivy had felt at ease with them all at once, had known that here were new friends and a new future, just waiting to be welcomed. They were offering her a cup of kindness, and she would take it with both hands.

By the crackling, log fire, Tom was curled, purring contentedly, black fur gleaming and green eyes winking, close to his new pal, Mabel.

"Happy New Year, you silly, dear old cat," Ivy whispered as Big Ben struck the 12th note, heralding the first day of their new beginnings. ■

She had no idea if she'd like him — or even if he'd
like her. All she did know was that nothing would
prevent her from keeping her . . .

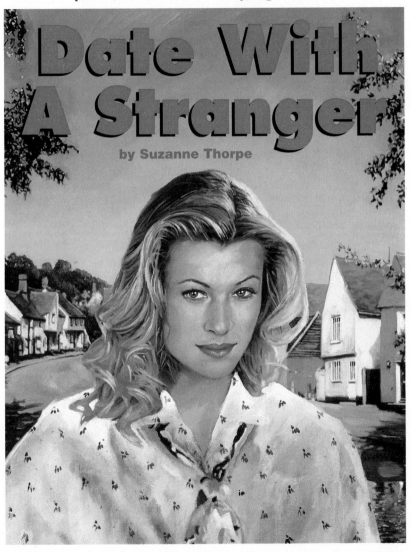

Date With A Stranger

by Suzanne Thorpe

"HE'LL like you — whatever you wear," her mother had reassured her.
But Ellie had to convince herself that she looked right — after all, she
had waited a very long time for this date.

What should she wear though? She mustn't try to look too sophisticated or even too casual, so jeans were out. She didn't want to give the wrong impression, nor did she want to risk unnerving him — or herself for that matter.

"Just be yourself," her mother had advised. "He'll want to get to know the real you."

"Will he now?" Ellie had retorted a little sharply. "I wish *I* knew the real me . . ."

And so after trying every possibility in her wardrobe, she finally ended up choosing her smart, tweed trousers and the new blouse she'd bought at Christmas time.

There — she was as ready as she'd ever be and glad they had agreed to meet at the restaurant.

Glad — until she arrived, that is.

HER legs felt like a rag doll's, and her brain seemed to be spinning inside her head.

What on earth would they say to each other . . . ? And as her mind struggled to find an answer another more frightening thought struck her.

What did he look like now . . . ?

"Ellie . . . ?" The voice was warm, the tone deep, slightly hesitant.

She turned and just *knew* it was him. Something inside her stirred, as she looked at him, long and searchingly.

He stepped forward and offered his hand. She took it in hers, appreciating his firm reassuring grip. She looked up into warm brown eyes.

"I've booked a table . . ." He gestured for her to walk through to the restaurant. "I wasn't sure if this was the right sort of place to bring you. I hope you like fish! Would you care for a drink?"

A bizarre quip cartwheeled through her mind — about drinking *like* a fish. She repressed it.

He sounded nervous, too.

"Yes, please," she replied. "White wine would be nice and yes — I do like fish." She smiled, as confidently as possible.

She pretended to skim the menu, aware of his gaze upon her. "Am I like you'd imagined?" he enquired, caution in his voice, intrigue in his eyes. She looked across at him, a little shyly.

"Yes and no, really. I didn't really know what to expect."

Ellie lowered her eyes, just a little embarrassed by her own awkwardness.

For he *was* what she expected — even hoped for — with those dark eyes that crinkled at the corners as if he smiled a lot. But he was older than she'd imagined.

"And me?" she asked, fixing him with eyes as blue as his were dark, only larger and more hopeful. He smiled, she thought, rather wistfully.

"Oh, you're lovelier than I could ever have imagined!" And the look he gave her, a sort of sad longing, made her eyes fill with tears.

166

Quickly she buried her face in the menu, blindly scanning the mouth-watering items again.

She continued the supposed scrutiny until she'd composed herself once more. At last she glanced up and, looking steadily at him over the table, she confessed:

"I don't think I can eat a thing! I'd no idea I could feel so nervous!"

He smiled encouragingly — a confident smile this time, full of promise.

"Shall I choose for us both, then? How about some fresh Scottish salmon . . . with a selection of salads — does that sound OK?"

Ellie nodded happily, her face breaking into a soft, pretty smile. He seemed to know just how to handle things although he must have been feeling just as tense as she was.

Suddenly she felt herself beginning to relax in the company of this attractive stranger.

I NEVER thought I'd manage all that," Ellie said with a contented sigh as she finished off the last mouthful of chocolate fudge cake. She realised he was watching her with warm amusement.

"There's so much I want to know about you, Ellie," he said, suddenly serious.

"Me, too — about you, I mean!" Ellie urged. He stirred his coffee thoughtfully before going on.

"Well . . . I'm just an over-worked accountant. I live in a nice apartment. I play golf, enjoy spy novels and crosswords — although I'm not all that good at them! I like woollen socks in black and navy, plain ties — oh . . . and I'm a sucker for animals — especially sad-eyed labradors!"

Ellie laughed for the first time that evening. It felt good.

"So, you see," he said, feigning a frown. "I'm really terribly boring!"

But Ellie pulled a playful and reproachful face at that, thinking to herself how lovely he was. Like a big comfortable armchair, a little frayed at the edges perhaps, but one she would love to curl into on rainy days and lonesome nights.

"Your turn, now. Tell me all about yourself . . ."

"I don't know where to start . . ."

"From the very beginning — please," he almost pleaded. She understood what he meant, knew what he wanted to hear, and took a deep steadying breath.

"I was only a tot when Mum's divorce came through, so I don't remember those early years much at all. Mum's always tried to make up for the fact there's just her.

"In fact, she probably went too far the other way — encouraged me to

167

try lots of different hobbies — ballet, horse-riding, playing the cello — you know, all the usual stuff. But I loved it all, and so it didn't really matter."

"But how did you feel about the divorce?" he asked.

"I understood," Ellie said simply. "Maybe not when I was really young but when I was older, in my teens I did.

Mum explained she had married too young, when she was still at university. It must have been difficult to study and work at a marriage at the same time —," Ellie mused, "— especially with a small baby . . ."

He looked down into his coffee, his thoughts private as Ellie continued.

"But I admire my parents — both of them." That made him look up quizzically.

"Well," she explained, "they admitted they'd made a big mistake in marrying when neither knew what they really wanted out of life — they had the courage to end their relationship, no hanging on unhappily together because of me. Anyway, I'm glad they split up on good terms."

She paused for a moment, looking at his handsome, attentive face.

"Perhaps Mum wanting a clean break was a bit selfish — and it made things harder for her in some ways, but she always says she doesn't have too many regrets."

"There's . . . there's no blame then?" he asked, his voice a little unsteady.

"None," Ellie said.

He nodded, as if he understood, then lowered his gaze to his coffee again.

A DEEP silence fell between them like a curtain, and Ellie felt suddenly lost and a little fearful. She recalled a similar feeling, once as a child when the night-light went out, leaving her lying alone in bed, in the dark.

"I'm a secretary," she went on quickly — trying to reach out to him in the silence. He looked up, attentive again, his private thoughts pushed aside for the moment.

"Well, personal assistant really, for a property developer. He thinks I'm the original Tinkerbell — able to flit from place to place, performing feats of magic as I go!"

He laughed and she welcomed the sound.

"And no doubt he's the original Peter Pan?"

She laughed back. "Well, yes. I suppose he is . . . Actually he's over fifty but looks much younger, how did you know?"

He smiled — almost boyishly.

"Because there's a Peter Pan lurking in here too, beneath this grey thatch!"

"Well, I'll see what I can do to coax him out," Ellie promised with an impish smile. Then he was serious again, his brows drawn together, the light-hearted moment over.

"Go on," he encouraged. "I want to know everything." Ellie shrugged, then plunged on.

168

"Well, apart from my job which I do enjoy, I like dancing and all kinds of music. I play tennis, adore clothes, have two cats, six pot plants . . ." She paused to ask, "Am I rabbitting on too much?"

"Not at all," he replied. "Is there a steady boyfriend, Ellie — anyone special?"

Ellie looked evasive.

"Sorry," he apologised, "none of my business."

"He's called Michael," Ellie replied, "and he works in an insurance office."

"Well, he's certainly a lucky young man —"

"Oh, I keep *telling* him that!" They both laughed, this time the same laugh.

Then a red-sleeved arm lowered a plate to the table. It was the bill — and it stopped their laughter like a red flag.

"Will we do . . . do this again?" Ellie asked, catching her breath.

"I'd certainly like to very much," he said gently, and she knew he meant it.

HE dropped her off at the flat, but before she opened the car door he tenderly reached out one slender, well-shaped finger to touch her chin. Then turning her gently to face him, he stared deeply into her eyes for a seemingly endless moment, as if hungry for her thoughts.

She had been miles away thinking how her life had changed such a lot in just two weeks since her mother had told her the news.

"There's someone over from Canada who wants to meet you, but it's up to you whether you want to meet him . . ."

And up until that day, two weeks ago, Paul Villiers had just been an old snapshot she hadn't been able to judge too clearly. He had been the missing piece in the jigsaw of her life.

Now she felt slightly insecure under his intense gaze.

"I still feel a little strange in your company . . ." Ellie confessed, lowering her dark fringe of lashes. Then she looked up, her eyes sparkling with hope. "But in other ways I feel so close to you —" she confided, "as if I've always known you."

He smiled tenderly, sadly . . . "You have. There's a bond between us which can never be broken. And we'll build on it, Ellie — I hope we'll always be good friends."

"I hope so, too," she whispered softly.

Then he kissed her on the forehead — lightly and tenderly. She felt a world of love pass between them. And as she ran up the steps to her front door, she felt ecstatic with her new found love — excited, round-eyed and five years old again.

And most of all she felt complete. For it wasn't every day a girl met her father. ■

SID'S SPECIAL

by Jilly
Brown

GIFT

What could an old codger like him give this new baby — except perhaps a piece of the past?

SIDNEY CARTER'S craggy old face beamed with pleasure as he carefully propped the precious blue envelope behind the white china cat on the mantel shelf.

It contained a lovely letter from his granddaughter announcing the birth of her baby and a beautiful photo of his new great-granddaughter.

Feeling proud and happy, he settled back in his old rocking-chair with his newspaper and reached for his early morning mug of tea.

However, as he raised the mug to his lips, the feeling of contentment faded a little.

What could he get as a gift for the baby, he pondered?

171

He sighed deeply. The trouble was, he was no good at this sort of thing. He'd always left that to Nellie. And it went without saying, this gift had to be something extra special.

After all, Lucy was his precious only granddaughter and they'd become even closer when Nellie had suddenly taken ill, just seven short months ago.

It didn't seem fair, that Nellie couldn't be here now to share this special event with him. He sighed again.

Those had been bleak days last winter when he just couldn't visualise a future without his Nellie.

It occurred to him that it was Lucy who'd finally lifted those dark clouds. Lucy, who'd unexpectedly brought some sunshine back into his life.

He remembered especially one afternoon Lucy had sat in Nellie's old rocker, and whispered tearfully, "I don't know what it is, Gramps, but I always feel so close to Nan sitting here in her old chair . . ."

After that he realised his beloved granddaughter was right. Often, sitting there, he felt as if Nellie was still with him. She smiled at him from the sideboard, her brown eyes twinkling from the silver frame.

And instead of tears filling his eyes, a smile would begin to play around his mouth as he remembered moments from their life . . .

WHEN Lucy had married Peter two years ago, Nellie had bought several metres of crisp white cotton fabric at the market and transformed that plain piece of material into an exquisite hand-embroidered table cloth.

Nellie would have made something special for baby Rachel's gift with her own small, capable hands, he knew that.

Nellie's hands had rarely been still. If she wasn't sewing, she was crocheting or knitting. Her needles flying so fast, as she watched TV in the evenings, that Sid had sometimes expected sparks instead of stitches.

Again his eyes flickered to the framed photo of Nellie as he wrestled with his problem. There were a few pounds worth of twenty pences tucked away by Nellie in the old tea caddy, but he knew there wasn't nearly enough for an expensive gift.

Half-heartedly he'd looked in a few shop windows whenever he'd been at the shops but nothing had caught his eye.

By the end of the week, he was beginning to panic. Only a week until Lucy was due to visit. He would have to have something to give this great granddaughter of his by then . . .

How he wished Nellie was still here, so that he could talk things over with her . . .

Then he smiled suddenly, a twinkle in his old eyes, for he knew full well what Nellie would have said to him.

So you're finally finding out for yourself how much things cost, Sidney Carter!

Right from the day they were married, he mused, Nellie had always been a great bargain hunter and a wonderful juggler of money.

That was the reason Sid had never had to bother his head about household management. For Nellie's thrifty ways had been completely reliable.

She'd always managed to provide tasty food for the table clothes on the family's backs and tobacco money in his pocket. And she'd still been able to put a little away for those special occasions — like now.

He wasn't very good at that sort of thing — in fact, he was downright hopeless.

Nellie's assessment of the situation came to him again, quite brusquely this time.

C'mon now Sid, stop all that wallowing in self pity, do you hear? You'll solve nothing sitting there brooding . . . it's high time you did something constructive . . .

Easier said than done, he thought, puffing away on his pipe, and thinking back to his disastrous trip to town earlier that day.

A display of colourful teddy-bears had caught his eye in the window of the big toy store but when he'd gone inside to have a closer look, he'd been disappointed and dismayed at the high prices he couldn't possibly afford.

Suddenly Sid was roused from his thoughts by Shep, his black and white collie, who was pushing his cold nose into Sid's hand, his tail wagging hopefully.

"Time for a walk, is it?" Sid grinned, knocking out his pipe.

He sighed as he put on his outdoor shoes. "I'm at a complete loss, Shep lad. Nellie was right about me, always having my head stuck up in the clouds. I miss her something terrible. Don't you, Shep?"

Shep wagged his tail in agreement. During the seven years of his life, Nellie had given the dog the sharp side of her tongue in the same way she'd given her love and affection — in great dollops.

And it was obvious Shep missed her, too . . .

Sid thought the walk might do him some good; clear his head, and make way for fresh thoughts — for the problem of Rachel's gift was beginning to weigh heavily on his mind.

L ATER that evening, while he was sitting in his rocker,   warming himself by the fire, after his walk, Nellie's rocker sat opposite him, empty and still.

The silence in the room was broken by the gas fire hissing in the hearth and the rain now splattering against the window panes.

"Hope the weather picks up for Lucy's visit," Sid muttered, his hands fondling Shep's ears.

Feeling snug and cosy in his little cottage sitting-room, Sid lit up his pipe and rested his feet comfortably on the hearth. As he puffed away contentedly, he thought, they've lasted well, these old chairs . . .

Through half-closed eyes, his mind drifted back . . . remembering how

173

he'd bought them from his Uncle Joe, over half a century ago, for two bob .

He could just see Nellie then, her long black wavy hair like a curtain around her lovely young face. She'd gently rocked, first Helen (Lucy's mum) then Tom, and finally young Michael . . . yes, she'd done her share of nursing in that old chair, Sid thought fondly.

He sighed. Looking back, it seemed no time at all before Nellie, flecks of grey showing in the beautiful dark hair, was rocking baby Lucy . . .

Babies were finally replaced by those clacking knitting needles and Nellie's old sewing basket.

The chairs were scratched and dull now — the pink and cream upholstery old and shabby. Nellie had intended recovering the cushions; making new ones. Just before she passed away.

Tears suddenly filled Sid's eyes. And one trickled down his cheek as he bent forward to knock out his pipe on the hearth.

Sid gave a little sigh. He wasn't ready for climbing the steep stairs to the chilly bedroom above. He'd just sit here awhile and think.

As he half-dozed, pictures of the kids playing and clambering on the rocking-chair danced before his eyes. How they'd all loved it . . .

Suddenly Sid jerked awake.

He was still sitting in his old rocker, his faithful old dog lay by his feet.

The wind and rain had died away. It seemed to him Nellie's chair was actually rocking. He shook his head, dismissing the thought.

"Come on, Shep, old son.

It's time we headed upstairs. Sleeping by the fireside plays funny tricks on the mind," he muttered.

S ID slept late the following morning. But when he finally pulled back the curtains, sunshine spilled into the room. He whistled cheerfully to himself as he pottered about getting himself ready.

He'd just made himself a tasty breakfast and was reaching for the paper when a brilliant idea flashed into his mind.

"I've got it, Shep! I think I've got it, lad!" he yelled excitedly.

And he jumped up and danced a little jig in his slippered feet.

Shep barked madly, while Sid took Nellie's jar of twenty-pence pieces from the back of the sideboard, emptied them out on the table and counted them.

This time when he went into town, he came back whistling and in high spirits. He'd managed to buy almost everything he needed from the big DIY store — and he still had a few twenty pences left.

"Best do this in the shed, Shep old son." He grinned mischievously.

Shep, tail wagging in agreement, followed Sid down to the bottom of the garden.

For the next few days, Sid was extremely busy. He whistled cheerfully while he worked, so engrossed that he didn't notice the cold conditions of his work place.

First thing on Saturday morning, he brought the old rocking-chair back

174